His Names, His Glories

Chinmaya Mahima

THE mananam SERIES

His Names, His Glories

Chinmaya Mahima

CHINMAYA PUBLICATIONS
CHINMAYA MISSION WEST PUBLICATIONS DIVISION

Chinmaya Publications
560 Bridgetown Pike, Feasterville Trevose, PA 19053-7240, USA
(215) 396-0390
www.chinmayapublications.com

Chinmaya Mission West
P.O. Box 129, Piercy, CA 95587, USA (707) 247-3488
www.chinmayamission.org

Central Chinmaya Mission Trust
Sandeepany Sadhanalaya
Saki Vihar Road
Mumbai 400 072, India
www.chinmayamission.com

Editorial Team
Editorial Advisors: Swami Shantananda, Swami Ishwarananda
Communication with the authors and
procuring articles: Neelima Polam
Series Editors: Shuba Sriram & Vidya Narayanan
Editorial Team: Aparna Kotapati, Maureen McIver,
Vidya Ramraj, Shilpi P. Reddy
Book cover artwork: Susheel Mantha
Book cover design & book layout: Shuba Sriram
Production & Distribution Manager: Lalet Sharma

Library of Congress Control Number: 2024937542
ISBN: 978-1-608-27038-5

Printed in the United States of America

Contents

Preface xvi
Swami Dheerananda

REFLECTIONS ON PŪJYA GURUDEV'S 108 NĀMAS

1. Om Ajāya Namaḥ 2
Swami Tejomayananda
Former Global Head of Chinmaya Mission

2. Om Avyayāya Namaḥ 4
Swami Swaroopananda
Global Head of Chinmaya Mission

3. Om Avināśine Namaḥ 6
Swami Shantananda
President, Chinmaya Mission West

4. Om Acintyāya Namaḥ 8
Swami Ishwarananda
Chinmaya Mission Los Angeles

5. Om Aprameyāya Namaḥ 10
Swamini Gangananda
Central Chinmaya Mission Trust

6. Om Advitīyāya Namaḥ 12
Swami Brahmananda
Chinmaya Mission Bengaluru

7. Om Aniketāya Namaḥ 14
Swami Abhayananda
Chinmaya Mission Thiruvananthapuram

8. Om Anuśāsanapriyāya Namaḥ 16
Swami Shrikarananda
Chinmaya Mission Australia

9. Om Antaḥsākṣiṇe Namaḥ 18
Brahmacharini Ananya Chaitanya
Chinmaya Mission Guwahati

10. Om Antaryāmine Namaḥ 20
Swami Sughoshananda
Chinmaya Mission Goa

11. Om Ānandāya Namaḥ 22
Swami Adityananda
Chinmaya Mission Mandya

12. Om Ātmasvarūpāya Namaḥ 24
Swami Shashvatananda
Chinmaya Mission Hosur

13. Om Ānglabhaṣāviduttamāya Namaḥ 28
Swami Dheerananda
Chinmaya Mission Washington Regional Center

14. Om Īśvarāya Namaḥ 30
Swami Viviktananda
Chinmaya Mission Kasargod

15. Om Udārahṛdayāya Namaḥ 32
Swami Sharanananda
Chinmaya Mission Chicago

16. Om Utsāhavardhakāya Namaḥ 34
Swami Chidatmananda
Chinmaya Mission Hyderabad

17. Om Ekasmai Namaḥ 36
Swami Advayananda
Central Chinmaya Mission Trust

18. Om Omkāravide Namaḥ 38
Swamini Shivapriyananda
Chinmaya Mission Toronto

19. Om Karuṇāsāgarāya Namaḥ 40
Swami Abhedananda
Chinmaya Mission South Africa

20. Om Karmaparāyaṇāya Namaḥ 42
Swamini Umananda
Chinmaya Mission France

21. Om Kālātītāya Namaḥ 44
Swami Chidrupananda
Chinmaya Mission Noida

22. Om Kaivalyasvarūpāya Namaḥ 46
Swamini Kaivalyananda
Central Chinmaya Mission Trust

23. Om Kṛtātmane Namaḥ 48
Swami Shuddhananda
Chinmaya Mission Port Blair

24. Om Kṛtakṛtyāya Namaḥ 50
Swami Sharadananda
Chinmaya International Foundation

25. Om Gītā-jñāna-yajña-pracārakāya Namaḥ 54
Swamini Radhikananda
Chinmaya Mission New Jersey

26. Om Gurave Namaḥ 56
Swami Mitrananda
Chinmaya Mission Chennai

27. Om Guṇātītāya Namaḥ 58
Swami Prakarshananda
Chinmaya Mission Delhi

28. Om Granthakṛte Namaḥ 60
Swami Avyayananda
Chinmaya Mission Gurugram

29. Om Cinmayāya Namaḥ 62
Swami Turiyananda
Chinmaya Mission Kadapa

30. Om Chinnasaṁśayāya Namaḥ 64
Swami Swatmananda
Chinmaya Mission Juhu

31. Om Jagadātmane Namaḥ 66
Vilasini Balakrishnan
Chinmaya Mission Washington Regional Center

32. Om Jagat-sākṣiṇe Namaḥ 68
Swami Aparajitananda
Chinmaya Mission Chicago

33. Om Janapriyāya Namaḥ 70
Swami Advaitananda
Chinmaya Mission Nashik

34. Om Jitendriyāya Namaḥ 72
Swamini Anukoolananda
Chinmaya International Residential School

35. Om Jīvabrahmaikyavide Namaḥ 74
Swami Aparokshananda
Chinmaya Mission Perth

36. Om Jīvanmuktāya Namaḥ 76
Swami Devatmananda
Chinmaya Mission Tapovan Kuti Ashram

37. Om Jīrṇa-mandira-uddhārakāya Namaḥ 80
Swami Gunatitananda
Chinmaya Mission Colombo

38. Om Tapovanaśiṣyāya Namaḥ 82
Dev Singh
Chinmaya Mission Toronto

39. Om Tapasvine Namaḥ 84
Swami Prakashananda
Chinmaya Mission Trinidad and Tobago

40. Om Tāpanāśanāya Namaḥ 86
Swami Ramakrishnananda
Chinmaya Mission Nagapattinam

41. Om Tīrthasvarūpāya Namaḥ 88
Brahmacharini Vrindha Chaitanya
Chinmaya Mission Jodhpur

42. Om Tejasvine Namaḥ 90
Brahmachari Anand Chaitanya
Chinmaya Mission Chennai

43. Om Dehātītāya Namaḥ 92
Swami Siddhananda
Chinmaya Mission Philadelphia

44. Om Dvandvātītāya Namaḥ 94
Swamini Aaradhanananda
Central Chinmaya Mission Trust

45. Om Dṛḍhaniścayāya Namaḥ 96
Swamini Sampratishtananda
Chinmaya Gardens, Coimbatore

46. Om Dharmasaṁsthāpakāya Namaḥ 98
Swamini Supriyananda
Chinmaya Mission Hong Kong

47. Om Dhīmate Namaḥ 100
Swamini Amritananda
Chinmaya Mission Nelson

48. Om Dhīrāya Namaḥ 102
Brahmacharini Robyn Thompson

49. Om Dhairyapradāya Namaḥ 106
Brahmachari Dvijot Chaitanya
Chinmaya Mission Guyana

50. Om Nārāyaṇāya Namaḥ 108
Brahmachari Hari Chaitanya
Chinmaya Mission Dallas

51. Om Nijānandāya Namaḥ 110
Brahmachari Soham Chaitanya
Chinmaya Mission San Jose

52. Om Nirapekṣāya Namaḥ 112
Brahmachari Sudheer Chaitanya
Chinmaya International Foundation

53. Om Niḥspṛhāya Namaḥ 114
Brahmachari Ved Chaitanya
Chinmaya International Foundation

54. Om Nirupamāya Namaḥ 116
Brahmacharini Aashraya
Chinmaya Mission Melbourne

55. Om Nirvikalpāya Namaḥ 118
Jaya Muzumdar
Chinmaya Mission Vancouver

56. Om Nityāya Namaḥ 120
Gina Singh
Chinmaya Mission Toronto

57. Om Nirañjanāya Namaḥ 122
Swami Atmavidananda
Chinmaya Mission Anantapur

58. Om Paramāya Namaḥ 124
Brahmacharini Jyoti Chaitanya
Chinmaya Mission Atlanta

59. Om Parabrahmaṇe Namaḥ 126
Brahmacharini Kritika Chaitanya
Chinmaya Mission Trinidad and Tobago

60. Om Pāvanāya Namaḥ 128
Brahmacharini Shripriya Chaitanya
Chinmaya Mission UK

61. Om Pāvakāya Namaḥ 132
Brahmacharini Shubhani Chaitanya
Chinmaya Mission New York

62. Om Puruṣottamāya Namaḥ 134
Brahmacharini Shweta Chaitanya
Chinmaya Mission West

63. Om Prasannātmane Namaḥ 136
Brahmacharini Stuti Chaitanya
Chinmaya Mission Columbus

64. Om Phalāsakti-rahitāya Namaḥ 138
Brahmacharini Taarini Chaitanya
Chinmaya International Foundation

65. Om Bahubhaktāya Namaḥ 140
Brahmacharini Divya
Chinmaya Mission Dallas

66. Om Bandha-mocakāya Namaḥ 142
Swamini Vimalananda
Chinmaya Gardens, Coimbatore

67. Om Brahmanisṭhāya Namaḥ 144
Brahmacharini Akalka
Chinmaya Mission New Jersey

68. Om Brahmaparāya Namaḥ 146
Swami Sivayogananda
Chinmaya Mission Madurai

69. Om Bhayanāśanāya Namaḥ 148
Aroona Kanhai
Chinmaya Mission Trinidad and Tobago

70. Om Bhāratagauravāya Namaḥ 150
Arvind Bhagwat
Chinmaya Mission Washington Regional Center

71. Om Bhūmne Namaḥ 152
Swamini Seelananda
Chinmaya Mission Ellayapalle

72. Om Mahavākyopadeśakāya Namaḥ 154
Dr. B.K. Sathyanarayana
Chinmaya Mission Washington Regional Center

73. Om Maharṣaye Namaḥ 158
Swami Raghuveerananda
Chinmaya Mission Vishakapatnam

74. Om Madhurasvabhāvāya Namaḥ 160
Swami Raghavananda
Chinmaya Mission Chas

75. Om Manoharāya Namaḥ 162
Swami Atmadevananda
Chinmaya Seva Trust, Maharashtra

76. Om Mahātmane Namaḥ 164
Raghu Grandige
Chinmaya Mission Atlanta

77. Om Medhāvine Namaḥ 166
Gaurang Nanavaty
Chinmaya Mission Houston

78. Om Yatātmane Namaḥ 168
Geetha Grandige
Chinmaya Mission Atlanta

79. Om Yajñakṛte Namaḥ 170
Swami Atulananda
Central Chinmaya Mission Trust

80. Om Lokaprasiddhāya Namaḥ 172
Swamini Gahanananda
Chinmaya Mission Tumkur

81. Om Vāgmine Namaḥ 174
Swami Prabuddhananda
Chinmaya Mission Indore

82. Om Vibhave Namaḥ 176
Jetindra Kumar Nayar
Chinmaya Mission Twin Cities

83. Om Vinodapriyāya Namaḥ 178
Kuntimaddi Sadananda
Chinmaya Mission Washington Regional Center

84. Om Vinayaśīlāya Namaḥ 180
Brahmacharini Pranati Chaitanya
Chinmaya Mission Ghaziabad

85. Om Vītarāgāya Namaḥ 184
Mahadevan Parameswaran
Chinmaya Mission Los Angeles

86. Om Vedāntavedyāya Namaḥ 186
Medha Bhagwat
Chinmaya Mission Washington Regional Center

87. Om Śāntāya Namaḥ 188
Swami Suveerananda
Chinmaya Mission Guntur

88. Om Śāntipradāya Namaḥ 190
Priya Kumar Maini
Chinmaya Mission Austin

89. Om Śāstroddhārakāya Namaḥ 192
Swami Vijayananda
Chinmaya Mission Vizianagaram

90. Om Śuddhasattvāya Namaḥ 194
Rahul Maini
Chinmaya Mission Austin

91. Om Śrutipāragāya Namaḥ 196
Brahmacharini Maitreyi Chaitanya
Chinmaya Mission Pune

92. Om Śrotriyāya Namaḥ 198
Sharada Kumar
Chinmaya Mission Ann Arbor

93. Om Sannyāsine Namaḥ 200
Shashi Duraiswami
Chinmaya Mission Washington Regional Center

94. Om Samabuddhaye Namaḥ 202
Shashikala Dwarakanath
Chinmaya Mission Boston

95. Om Saccidānandāya Namaḥ 204
Siva Velu
Chinmaya Mission Alpharetta

96. Om Sarvahitacintakāya Namaḥ 206
Sukanya Sathya
Chinmaya Mission Washington Regional Center

97. Om Satyasaṅkalpāya Namaḥ 210
Suresh Ramakrishnan
Chinmaya Mission Washington Regional Center

98. Om Santuṣṭāya Namaḥ 212
Sushma Siva
Chinmaya Mission Alpharetta

99. Om Sādhave Namaḥ 214
Swapna Nayar
Chinmaya Mission Twin Cities

100. Om Sumanase Namaḥ 216
Brahmacharini Vaani I. Ramkhalawan
Central Chinmaya Mission Trust

101. Om Suhṛde Namaḥ 218
Swami Deveshananda
Chinmaya Mission Vadodara

102. Om Svayaṁ-jyotiṣe Namaḥ 220
Veena Venkatesh
Chinmaya Mission Phoenix

103. Om Sthitaprajñāya Namaḥ 222
Venkatesh Hollabbi
Chinmaya Mission Phoenix

104. Om Kṣamāśīlāya Namaḥ 224
Vijay Gupta
Chinmaya Mission London

105. Om Jñānamūrtaye Namaḥ 226
Vijay Kumar
Chinmaya Mission Washington Regional Center

106. Om Jñānayogine Namaḥ 228
Swami Nirbhayananda
Chinmaya Mission Vasai

107. Om Jñānatṛptāya Namaḥ 230
Swami Sarvagananda
Chinmaya Mission Vijayawada

108. Om Nitya-śuddha-buddha-mukta svarūpāya Namaḥ 232
Vivek Gupta
Chinmaya Mission Niagara &
Chinmaya Mission Cleveland

Transliteration and Pronunication Guide 236

Preface

Chinmaya! The light of Consciousness that illumines all our experiences – physical, emotional, and intellectual, in all three states – waking, dream, and deep sleep, is our glorious Guru, Swami Chinmayananda!

Meeting the Master is indeed love at first sight!

His brilliance, compassion, and divine life kindle our hearts, inspire us, and keep us on the path of virtue, courage, and wisdom!

Our Guru is indeed Chinmaya Kṛṣṇa, who imparted the life-transforming teachings of the *Bhagavad-gītā* and thereby sparked the Hindu Renaissance worldwide!

Our Guru is indeed Brahman – The Supreme Reality! Therefore, His Glories are immeasurable, incomprehensible, and inexplicable!

However, the Divine glories we experienced are indeed many!

- His exuberant eloquence!
- His determined discipline!
- His total fearlessness!
- His enchanting enthusiasm!
- His majestic military walk!
- His Divine form – the moving sacred place of pilgrimage for millions of devotees!
- And many, many more...

Each glory of Gurudev is an indication of His Divine Nature and an inspiration for us to contemplate upon and imbibe His glorious teachings.

Commemorating our Gurudev's 108th Jayanti, 108 Chinmaya Mission Vedānta Teachers across the world have shared their loving reflections on His 108 Divine Glories to inspire seekers to discover the Divine within.

1 – Consciousness alone shines!

0 – the non-apprehension of That One Consciousness, creates misapprehensions…

8 – the erroneous identification with the five senses, mind, intellect, and ego!

To apprehend the '1' – Consciousness, Chinmaya, to remove the Non-apprehension, '0' – which creates misapprehensions, and to free ourselves from our erroneous identification with the five senses, mind, intellect, and ego, '8' – we invoke the divine Grace and blessings of our Gurudev with His 108 Divine Glories!

When we turn our alert and vigilant intellect's attention exclusively unto Him, the intellect is hushed and stultified! Then Gurudev's Mahāvākya reverberates –

"Last thought thoughted!
And no new thought thoughting!
The Divine merging happens!"

Cinmayam jagadīśvaram praṇamāmyaham!

~ Swami Dheerananda

divyo hyamūrtaḥ puruṣaḥ sabāhyābhyantaro hyajaḥ,
aprāṇo hyamanā śubhro hyakṣarāt parataḥ paraḥ.

Self-resplendent, formless, unoriginated and pure, that all-pervading Being is both within and without, anterior both to life and mind. He transcends even the transcendent, unmanifested, causal state of the Universe.

~ *Muṇḍakopaniṣad* 2.1.2

1

Om Ajāya Namaḥ

Salutations to the Unborn.

Swami Tejomayananda

Pūjya Gurudev's 108 names, like the other nāmāvalis, include some names indicating the formless and attribute-less Reality or Brahman, some indicating the Lord with attributes, called Īśvara in Vedānta, and some indicating a special manifestation with form and specific qualities.

The first name, 'ajaḥ', meaning 'Unborn' indicates Brahman – the beginningless supreme Truth. And that which is unborn is also immutable and indestructible.

Essentially, every jīva is 'ajaḥ', so why don't we worship everyone with this name? That is because greatness is not just in being but in knowing oneself to be beyond birth (and death). In the Bālakāṇḍa of *Śrī Rāmacaritamānasa* 22.3-4, Gosvāmī Tulasīdāsa says,

byāpak eku brahma abināsi,
sata chetan ghan ānandarāsi,
asa prabhu hṛdaya acata abikārī,
sakala jīva jaga dīna dukhārī.

"The all-pervading blissful Brahman resides in the heart of all beings, yet all beings are found to be suffering and sorrowful."

Then what is the use? Only when one realizes their Real Nature is Bliss Absolute will there be any benefit to being that Bliss!

So, there is 'being', and 'knowing'. And along with that, there has to be 'abidance' in the Self. In *Śrīmad Bhāgavatam's* second canto, we find the story of Ṛṣi Kardama and Devahūtī, who had the Lord Himself manifesting as their son – Kapila Muni. At His advent, Ṛṣi Kardama sang hymns in praise of the Lord and then sought permission to go to the forest to meditate. The Lord Himself has been born as his son, but he wanted to go away and meditate! Bhagavān Kapila also guided and blessed him, saying, "Go and meditate, and abide in your true Self." So, along with 'being' and 'knowing', 'abidance in the Self' is also very important.

The practical implication of this knowledge is that we become fearless. We can see a glimpse of such fearlessness in our Parama Gurudev Swami Tapovan Maharaj when Pūjya Gurudev wanted to take him to Delhi for treatment. Tapovan Maharaj asked, "Why? Do people not die in Delhi?" The body is born, and it will die when the time comes. But I was neither born nor will I ever die! Our Pūjya Gurudev's fearlessness also reflects His abidance in the unborn Self.

That which is born, changes, and dies is an object of the world. When I know from the scriptures that I am the unborn Self, I do not remain an object of the world. This clear experience is visible in Pūjya Gurudev's well-known quote, "Live in the world, but never be OF the world."

Thus, when we chant and contemplate this name with regular and sincere upāsanā (worship), we slowly rise to that level and remain unaffected by the ever-changing world. We realize our own Unborn, true Identity.

2

Om Avyayāya Namaḥ

Salutations to the imperishable.

Swami Swaroopananda

If we are unborn, then why and how does birth take place? What is its purpose? Of what use is the knowledge that I am unborn? How would we feel, and what would we do if we knew we were imperishable and unchanging? To prove that the Ātman, the Self, is eternal, Śrī Kṛṣṇa points out a direct means of inquiry, a method that leads us to discover the Truth here and now. Discover the Eternal – Now!

Śrī Kṛṣṇa asks us to analyze the body and how its matter undergoes continuous change. The childhood body that you had is not the youth or old-aged body that you have now. Every cell in the body dies and is replaced by other cells. But observe carefully. Don't you feel that you were the same child that you are now in your youth? Thus, when the body changes, you do not change. When the body dies, you do not die.

Therefore, avyaya is the indicator through which you try to recognize that which is unchanging and indestructible – the permanent You. By contemplating the words aja, avyaya, avināśine, you come to recognize that you are Unborn.

A month before His mahāsamādhi, Gurudev was in London. He had retired to His kuṭiyā, but the youngsters kept quizzing me with questions till well past 10:00 p.m. The next morning, Gurudev came out of His room, looking for me. The lady serving Him explained, "Swamiji went to bed quite late because the youth were hanging around, bombarding him with questions. He must be resting."

Gurudev turned to the youth and asked, "Why do you over-work my Swami and keep him up so late? If you have questions, why don't you ask me?"

The youngsters replied, "Gurudev, we didn't want to trouble you because you are unwell."

Precisely at that moment, I walked into the room. Gurudev exclaimed, "Do I look sick, or does he look sick!"

It was taboo to tell Him that He was sick. Despite what the doctors stated about His health, He was unchanged. He was a roaring lion. If we listen to the recordings of His first and last recorded talks – His strength, dynamism, enthusiasm, and love, remain unchanged, avyaya.

As we go deeper into Vedānta, we will recognize why and how the 'Unborn' takes birth. We will understand how Gurudev's life is an example of such an avatāra, such a manifestation. Avyaya means one who is eternal and beyond time. Even today, people recall Pūjya Gurudev's looks, skin texture, enthusiasm, and dynamism. A person as perfect as Gurudev, in all aspects – the way He walked, dressed, spoke – is ever imperishable.

When someone asked Gurudev to write His biography, He hilariously wrote, "Praised by many, criticized by some, I know not, but I continue to do my work."

His love, in every situation, was unchanging. His compassion, in every situation, was unchanging. However old His body may have become, and however sick we thought He may have been, He was unchanging – avyaya.

3

Om Avināśine Namaḥ

Salutations to the one who is indestructible.

Swami Shantananda

One of the most difficult fears to overcome is the fear of death. But the truth is that even the most powerful atomic bomb cannot destroy the Self.

Once, Sant Tukārām was approached by one of his devotees who asked, "Maharāj, how are you so cheerful, loving, and happy always? Please tell me the secret so that I, too, can be cheerful, loving, and happy." Sant Tukārām said, looking straight into the eyes of his devotee, "You are going to die in seven days!" This man was an ardent devotee and had total faith in the words of the Mahātmā. He returned home and started thinking that he only had seven days left and must use every moment to live properly. So, he started loving his wife, children, friends, and even his enemies. He wanted every moment to be the best. And so he decided to live and love to the fullest for the rest of the time he had left. Everyone around him was surprised and wondered about his transformation. Thus, he lived counting the days. And finally, the seventh day came. He rushed to Sant Tukārām, who calmly asked, "How were the last seven days?" The man replied, "I lived every moment loving everyone around me, and now I am ready to go." Sant Tukārām laughed and said, "You are not going anywhere. What I told you was the answer to your question. And that is exactly how I am happy and cheerful all the time. This is the secret. Once you know you are going to die anytime, you make use of every moment of your life to make it a meaningful one!"

acchedyo'yam adāhyo'yam akledyo'śoṣya eva ca,
nityaḥ sarva-gataḥ sthāṇuḥ acalo'yaṁ sanātanaḥ.

"The Consciousness is unbreakable and incombustible;
it can neither be dampened nor dried. It is everlasting,
in all places, unalterable, immutable, and primordial."
(Bhagavad-gītā 2.24)

Once a person realizes that he is that imperishable Truth, then what can death do to him? Death happens only to that which is born and that which identifies with the experiences of the body, the mind, and the intellect. That which is Unborn is changeless and doesn't die. Pūjya Gurudev Swami Chinmayananda realized that His Real Nature is that Consciousness – the changeless, imperishable Truth – Paramātmā; that which knows no destruction; that by which the entire world of names and forms are pervaded, and that which pervades and enlivens everything.

Pūjya Gurudev, though not here with us in His physical form, continues to be with us. He continues to be ever-present as that Paramātmā in each one of us, blessing us every moment. In fact, without His grace and blessings, it is impossible for anyone to perform any kind of activity.

4

Om Acintyāya Namaḥ

Salutations to the unthinkable.

Swami Ishwarananda

Cintā or worry is directionless thinking. When we are helpless about a situation and don't know what to do, we get into cintā or directionless thinking, which neither helps the situation nor provides a solution. Whereas cintanaṁ is focused thinking. When we reflect on the scriptures, we do systematic, purposeful thinking. Contemplation on Vedānta is called Vedānta-cintanaṁ, which is just the opposite of cintā!

The mind's nature is to oscillate. It is emotional, indecisive, restless, and constantly doubting itself. The intellect's work is to retain the gathered information, cyclically apply it in experiences, and learn from it. Unlike worldly knowledge, which has to be only perceived and thought of, understanding the nature of the Self requires one additional step beyond thinking – it has to be heard, thought of, and then meditated upon. Going beyond the buddhiḥ means understanding that realizing the Self is not a product of thinking. It is unthinkable – acintya.

Pūjya Gurudev has indicated that the Self, the pure Awareness, cannot be realized through the intellect. It is not only about being cognizant of what we do in the world but also about the ability to observe our thoughts and correct the course of thinking. Pure Awareness (prajñānaṁ) is not lost even if the mind stops thinking. Śrī Ādi Śankarācārya, in *Vivekacūḍāmaṇi* (169), pointed out that the world dissolves when the mind is absent and reappears in its presence. Then, who am I? Who is present when the mind functions or is absent? I am verily the pure Awareness – prajñānaṁ.

Even as Vedānta declares that Awareness cannot be thought of, some Upaniṣads perplexingly declare that it should be thought about and instruct us not to think about Awareness the way we do with the objects of the world. The masters compassionately explain that the instruction means pure Awareness should never be objectified. This is because objectifying anything inherently requires limiting it. A thought can be objectified only in one of four ways – using nāma (name), rūpa (form), guṇa (attribute), or karma (function). Pure Awareness is beyond all four, beyond the known realm. It is acintya.

To reach this state of Awareness, the great jñānis emulated the process of withdrawal in sleep, but with awareful attention on 'I am'. This is known as objectless awareness or dhyānam. Upaniṣads state that AUM is the greatest support for the seeker. Just as the three letters of AUM represent all sounds, the interspaced pure silence between two successive AUMs represents the realm beyond sounds. The journey of the seeker is from sound to no sound, from thought to no thought.

The initial practice in meditation should start with the utterance of AUM, then gradually shift attention to the silence between the AUMs, and eventually increase the duration of silence. When one can maintain the silence without the sound of AUM, the seeker abides in silence. So, too, between thoughts is the ever-present Awareness. Such a state of being is known as acintya, the state of uninterrupted abidance, where we can meet Pūjya Gurudev, who resides in everyone's heart as unthinkable pure Awareness!

5

Om Aprameyāya Namaḥ

Salutations to the immeasurable.

Swamini Gangananda

Truth is one and One alone, all-pervading, and one-without-a-second. Truth cannot be apprehended through any of the existing equipment of body, mind, and intellect. Nothing can be added to It or deducted from It; nameless, formless, qualityless but addressed with countless names. In Vedānta, it is said that these countless names indicate the same Truth. There are thousands of names composed by numerous devotees in praise of different Gods. They are all nothing but indicators of the supreme Reality, the Truth. The indicators, however, are not That which is indicated.

To realize or merge in the supreme Reality, the Truth, equipments like the body, mind, and intellect are to be mobilized to a single point by karma yoga, bhakti yoga, and jñāna yoga. A true devotee or a disciple should consider their Guru as Brahman Itself to release themselves from the bondage of karma or birth and death. (*Bhagavad-gītā* 7.17) says 'jñāni eka bhaktir viśiṣyate'. A jñāni has one Guru, one God, and one mantra. Those whipped by worldly desires run after many Gods and Gurus (*Bhagavad-gītā* 7.20). The state of perfection is to attain freedom from the bondage of karma (birth and death).

This state of perfection is attained by proper method of worship and can be possible for the one who dedicates himself "to That from which everything proceeds, by Which everything is pervaded" (*Bhagavad-gītā* 18.45-46). "I am easily attainable by that ever steadfast one who constantly remembers only Me daily, not anything else" (*Bhagavad-gītā* 8.14).

There are the waking, dream, and deep sleep states of consciousness. Dissociate with all of them, what remains is pure Consciousness. There are no words to describe It. Beyond past, present, and future, It alone was, is, and will be.

That space, which is subtle and all-pervading, cannot be measured. To measure space, one has to separate oneself from space, which is impossible. The supreme Brahman pervades in and through space. "This whole universe is pervaded by My unmanifested form" (*Bhagavad-gītā* 9.4). All this is pervaded by Īśa (*Īśāvāsya-upaniṣad* 1). So, measuring supreme Reality with scientific measurements is not possible!

This Reality is invoked through Pūjya Gurudev's name, "Om aprameyāya namaḥ" – Salutations to the Immeasurable. The pādukās are small, but the lakṣya or what they symbolize, is more important, "nikṛṣṭa vastu utkṛṣṭa dṛṣṭi." The Advaita philosophy – jīvātmā is Paramātmā (tat tvam asi) – is only found in Vedānta, not in any other religious texts. Śrī Ādi Śankarācārya and Swami Chinmayananda emphasized it without ignoring Rāmāyaṇa, Mahābhārata, Purāṇas, or other devotional texts. When it is said that 'jīvātmā is Paramātmā' or 'tat tvam asi', it is the lakṣyārtha (the indirectly expressed meaning). When the conditions and qualities are removed from both jīvātmā and Paramātmā there remains only the supreme Reality.

6

Om Advitīyāya Namaḥ

Salutations to the One without a second.

Swami Brahmananda

There was a time when the *Bhagavad-gītā* was considered a holy scripture fit to be kept only in one's pūjā room. Once in a while, the chanting of some verses would be heard on ākāśavāṇī (All India Radio), mostly whenever a politician or a person of national importance died. None bothered to know what the chanting meant.

It was Pūjya Gurudev who declared to the world that the *Bhagavad-gītā* was not 'maraṇa' *gītā,* a song for the dead, but a song for the living man; it is a 'man-making' *Gītā*. Through His *Gītā* jñāna-yajña, Gurudev made it clear how this scripture was helpful to all of us in our daily life of struggles, challenges, tragedies, and calamities. Gurudev thundered from His yajñaśālā, "This scripture can strengthen us, console us, inspire us, enlighten us, by helping us connect to the Divine in us."

Pūjya Gurudev was the first to give lectures on the scriptures in public places in English! Protests rose from various orthodox Hindu quarters. Some called it a sin and questioned how such holy, sacred teachings could be given to non-Hindus and non-Brahmins. Others complained, saying that these scriptures are written in deva-bhāṣā, Saṁskṛtam (the language of the Gods) and that it is blasphemous to give discourses on these scriptures in English, an inferior language. In addition, they also ridiculed the encouragement of women to study the Vedas and learn to chant the mantras from the Upaniṣads, saying that they go against the injunctions of the scriptures!

But Pūjya Gurudev, paying least attention to the prattling of the deluded orthodox fanatics, went ahead with His divine mission of spreading the knowledge of the scriptures, keeping in mind the parting advice of the Lord in the *Bhagavad-gītā* (18.69):

"Anyone who imparts this divine knowledge to My devotees is the dearest devotee of Mine. There is none who can render a greater service to Me."

Pūjya Gurudev not only imparted spiritual teachings but also established institutions like Sandeepany Sadhanalaya, where spiritual teachers are trained in different languages and sent to different parts of the world. In this sense, Pūjya Gurudev is one of the Lord's greatest devotees!

Prostrations unto such a spiritual Master, the One without a second, who made the scriptures accessible and easy to understand even for a layperson, created a Guru-śiṣya paramparā (lineage of teachers and students), ensuring an uninterrupted flow of Self-knowledge for the future generation and created a platform called Chinmaya Mission, thereby facilitating opportunities to learn, serve, love, and evolve.

"Awakening into that plane of non-dual Consciousness where one unquestionably determines that the Self in Him is the Self in all."
~ Swami Chinmayananda

7

Om Aniketāya Namaḥ

Salutations to the one who has no abode.

Swami Abhayananda

A real sannyāsī need not have a permanent settlement. Pūjya Gurudev traveled all around the world. His high degree of non-attachment helped Him not to consider anything, including the Chinmaya Mission, as His own. That is the extent of detachment Gurudev showed in all His worldly actions. Nārāyaṇa, or the realization of Brahman, is the final abode for everyone. Gurudev taught and experienced that higher Realm of the spiritual journey.

Pūjya Gurudev was born and brought up in Ernakulam. His mother passed away when he was a child. The young Balakrishnan Menon studied in Thrissur and stayed at his relative's home in the same town. He pursued his higher studies in Lucknow. He then became associated with the Indian freedom movement. His actions caught the attention of the British, who captured and tortured him in prison. One day, Balakrishnan lost consciousness, weakened by typhus and poor hygiene in prison. The British threw him on the roadside on the outskirts of the city and left him to die. The kindness of an Anglo-Indian lady saved his life. After recovering from the illness, Balakrishnan worked as a journalist in the National Herald. On one occasion, he wanted to expose the laziness of sannyāsins. In his skeptical view, the sādhus were parasites and a burden to civilized society. He started his journey to the Himalayas to unveil the 'ill habits of the so-called sādhus'. He chose Swami Sivananda's āśram for this purpose. Swami Sivananda's loving disposition towards the young seeker with an endlessly questioning mind woke up the sannyāsī inside the young Balakrishnan and made him the real aniketa. This was the beginning of Swami Chinmayananda's spiritual journey that soon led Him to Swami Tapovanam of Uttarkashi. With the grace and blessings of Swami Tapovanam and Mother Ganga, Pūjya Gurudev could endure the intense cold in Gangotri and Uttarkashi for more than two years to study the Vedānta texts under the tutelage of his Guru Swami Tapovanam.

From 1951 onwards, Pūjya Gurudev did hundreds of jñāna-yajñas. For more than four decades, the Vedānta Ganga flowed through Him to the world around Him. In those forty years, Gurudev stayed in thousands of residences and inspired lakhs of people worldwide. On most days, He woke up in a new place. He went through several geographical areas in different countries and continents. A real vairāgī (dispassioned) man cares least for his comfortable living. Due to Pūjya Gurudev's hectic schedule, He often ended up sleeping during on flights and trains. He lived as a homeless – aniketa – a real wandering monk and taught this incomparable knowledge to the common public. He chose San Diego, USA, to shed His mortal body. His samādhī took place in Sidhbari; His kuṭiyā is in Mumbai, and His vision center is in Pune, where the first yajña happened.

Even though His physical presence has not been with us, our beloved Gurudev resides in our hearts. One who realizes Brahman becomes Brahman. The all-pervading Brahman needs no particular place. He resides everywhere. We meditate on this quality of a Realized Master.

8

Om Anuśāsanapriyāya Namaḥ

Salutations to the one who loves discipline.

Swami Shrikarananda

To realize one's true Self, one needs to have citta-śuddhi (purity of mind) and citta-ekāgratā (single-pointedness of mind). But how does one acquire these qualities with a mind full of vāsanā expressions running everywhere? Discipline is required to tame, redirect, and strengthen the mind.

Gurudev was known to be a strict disciplinarian. He led by example. His discipline is doused in love because, as a Guru, He only wants our well-being and happiness. From His external appearance with crisply ironed clothes impeccably worn to His letters, which were carefully tailored to the recipient, Gurudev showed us that perfection is possible when every action is done with complete awareness and dedication.

Many of us have heard stories from our senior swāmins of their experiences while studying at Sandeepany Sadhanalaya in Powai. There was one such incident where Gurudev started teaching his early morning class, that went past breakfast time. The students were getting hungry. A devotee had brought a freshly harvested, big bunch of bananas. One hungry student took two bananas from the bottom, thinking that Gurudev would not find out. To his surprise, at the end of the class, Gurudev asked, "Who ate the two bananas?" No one came forward. Seeing this, Gurudev said, "Food is more important than Vedānta for all of you. So, today's lunch and dinner are canceled for all students." But Gurudev's tough love was never without compassion. Although Gurudev was diabetic and required timely meals, Gurudev instructed the cook not to prepare food for Him – "If my children don't eat, how can I?" He then instructed the cook to make an afternoon snack for all the students so they would not go hungry. Gurudev practiced discipline not out of ego but with love and a clear goal.

Despite being in a world of hustle and bustle and competing priorities rife with tardiness and untimeliness, Gurudev led the Mission by precedence. Every activity, however big or small, would start and end on time. Each one's time is valuable. Thus, when we are disciplined with time, each one feels valued.

Gurudev showed us that a disciplined mind must be diligently trained and lovingly nurtured. Gurudev carried His japa mālā with Him and would practice japa in quiet moments. He showed us that our mind must be kept alert, vigilant, and always in remembrance of the goal with regular practice of our sādhana.

Gurudev's every breath and action, is a lesson to all of us on how to integrate our mind and intellect for study, meditation, and finally, Realization. He showed and urged us, as His disciples and devotees, to live a life of discipline, which leads us to freedom. For me, this is why He is called anuśāsanapriya, and to Him, I surrender.

9

Om Antaḥ-sākṣiṇe Namaḥ

Salutations to the inner witness.

Brahmacharini Ananya Chaitanya

Who is a sākṣi? Just like we need a cell phone, sim card, and an app for mobile to connect, we need the trio of knowledge, knower, and known for any knowledge to take place. But to connect, they need a common platform. In the case of a mobile, the binary code becomes the common platform. Similarly, being the substratum of the trio, the sākṣi (Brahman) facilitates the fundamental connection for the knowledge to happen.

The sākṣi enlivens the inert sense organs, enabling them to act, and is also the substratum on which they act. In layman's language, sākṣi is the one who witnesses the various thoughts by enlivening the inert sense organs and says, "I have this experience."

Sākṣi does not have a form. Knowledge means forms. If sākṣi had a fixed form, it would be bound to that form. The fact that we all have sequential knowledge proves that sākṣi is dropping one form and taking another.

Taking it deeper, how can the formless sākṣi take any form? The forms appearing and disappearing on the sākṣi are mere illusions or superimpositions created like the light and sound show. There is no other reality existing other than the sākṣi. I can name that sākṣi as Lord, Guru, or Brahman.

In 2010, before becoming a brahmacāriṇi, I traveled

alone to Sidhbari by train to attend Pūjya Guruji Swami Tejomayananda's yajña. But on the way I was robbed of all my belongings except for some clothes. It was my first visit to Sidhbari, and I knew no one (except Gurudev). I had no phone or money and did not know who I could contact, as I didn't even have the address of the āśram!

While I stood gazing outside the door of the speeding train, I was getting the vibes of a parivrājaka-sannyāsi without food or belongings. At that moment, Gurudev spoke to me as antaḥsākṣi, "You belong to me. You are not alone." His voice was loud and clear. Unbelievably, when I got off the train, a tall and sturdy policeman came to assist me at Pathankot. After filing an FIR, the policeman contacted my mother and the āśram authorities and gave me 2000 rupees. He even arranged my transport. After reaching the āśram, one of the authorities gave me more money, and two others gave me two sets of brand-new phones with SIM cards. I got more than what I lost! My heart was yearning for more 'silent whispers' from my antaḥsākṣi Gurudev. After prostrating, I sat at His samādhi-sthal and started thanking Him profusely with an incessant gush of tears rolling down my face. The soothing quietness in front of Gurudev's samādhi lulled all my raging thoughts. The silence was so evident that I could even hear my breath. Suddenly, I heard the rustling sound of clothes, as if someone had entered wearing a dhoti. Becoming conscious of my tears, I slowly opened my eyes to see who had joined me at the samādhi-sthal. But lo! There was no one there. But I knew exactly who it was! My antaḥsākṣi Gurudev!

10

Om Antaryāmine Namaḥ

Salutations to the inner controller.

Swami Sughoshananda

Pūjya Gurudev Swami Chinmayananda was a śrotriya and a brahmaniṣṭha, one who is well versed in the scriptures as well as one who had the direct experience of Brahman as one's inner Self. Śāstras say, "brahmavit brahmaiva bhavati," the knower of the Self becomes the Self. Being Brahman, He also knows everything that is going on within and without Himself.

Om antaryāmine namaḥ: Salutations to the one who is the inner controller or one who controls from within – ante sthitvā yāmayati iti. Gurudev was an antaryāmī in the true sense. Many devotees who attended His lectures would be surprised to hear Him cite examples and anecdotes that happened in their lives. Before a person could ask a question, Pūjya Gurudev would have answered it in His lecture or satsaṅg. Someone once asked whether He could read minds. Gurudev humorously replied, "I have better things to do than to read your dirty mind!"

Antaryāmī also means one who has perfect control over his mind and senses. Scriptures say that those who have control over their mind can control the entire world, including the five elements (pañcamahābhūta).

Earlier, when Gurudev used to conduct spiritual camps at the Sidhbari Āśram in Himachal Pradesh, there was a practice to perform samaṣṭi Viṣṇusahasranāma pūjā and archana. In one such spiritual camp, preparations were going on for a big pūjā in the open ground. When everything was ready and the pūjā was about to start, all of a sudden, the entire climate changed as the rain clouds gathered over the āśram. Everyone panicked that everything would be washed off if it rains. At that time, Pūjya Gurudev, sitting in the open ground overseeing the pūjā arrangements, lifted His gaze toward the sky and started looking at the clouds as though commanding the wind (God) to move the clouds away. Within a few minutes, the sky was cleared of all the clouds, and the pūjā was conducted as per plan. However, as soon as the pūjā was over, it poured heavily. This incident shows that Pūjya Gurudev, as antaryāmī, could even control the natural forces.

It is said that our mind also remains under our control when we are in the company of a Mahātmā, and as soon as we move away from His company, the mind goes back to the mundane things (sense objects). This was the experience of many sādhakas who had the good fortune to be in the company of Pūjya Gurudev. Even today, when we travel to places like Sidhbari and the Sandeepany Sadhanalaya, we can feel Pūjya Gurudev's holy presence there, and our minds become calm effortlessly. May Pūjya Gurudev's blessings be upon us to control our minds and senses and fix them on our spiritual goal of liberation.

11

Om Ānandāya Namaḥ

Salutations to the blissful one.

Swami Adityananda

In our heritage, several aṣṭottara śata nāmāvalis have been composed glorifying deities and Gurus. Every nāma in these nāmāvalis denotes pure Consciousness. We can also consider these names as our own identity. We are, in reality, pure Consciousness alone. The 108 names composed on Pūjya Gurudev Swami Chinmayananda also follow the same tradition.

'Om ānandāya namaḥ' is the eleventh name in the aṣṭottara śata nāmāvali of Pūjya Gurudev. Śrī Ādi Śankarācārya has enquired about the nature of ātmā in *Tattva Bodha* and explains it as 'saccidānanda svarūpa' (Sat – Existence, Cit – Knowledge, Ānanda – Bliss). Here, Gurudev is represented as the form of bliss. Gurudev always had a smiling face. This bliss is beyond happiness and sorrow. Happiness and sorrow come one after the other like the waves of water in an ocean.

When we stay grounded in Bliss, we become a mere witness to the appearance and disappearance of happiness and sorrow. We are blissful in sleep totally ignorant of our bodies. When we wake up, we get identified with the body and its attributes, such as male or female, and start playing the roles of brother, sister, father, mother, and so on. When we forget our true nature, we wrongly identify with what we are not and start playing different roles experiencing happiness and sorrow.

In *Maitreya-upaniṣad* belonging to the Sāma Veda, Lord Śiva says,

dhanavṛddhā vayovṛddhā vidyāvṛddhāstathaiva ca,
te sarve jñānavṛddhasya kinkarāḥ śiṣyakinkarāḥ.

"In this world, there are people who have acquired wealth and become old. While many have become old just by age, others have acquired worldly knowledge and are old knowledge-wise. All of these people become disciples and servants of the wise man who has attained the knowledge of Brahman."

The rich, the old, the learned, and the scientists used to meet Gurudev. All of them saw in Gurudev the embodiment of Self-knowledge. His personality, always floating in the ocean of bliss, became a beacon for all sādhakas.

A doctor gave an apple to Pūjya Gurudev and said that an apple a day keeps the doctor away. Gurudev gave it back to him as prasād and said, "Don't ever give it to your wife." This was Gurudev's wit and humor. Thus, the name 'om ānandāya namaḥ' befittingly suits Gurudev as He was always immersed in the ocean of Ānanda – Bliss.

When we practice the prescribed spiritual practices, our life will also be blissful like that of Gurudev. As Śrī Ādi Śankarācārya said in the commentary of the *Bhagavad-gītā*, 'sthitaprajñasya lakshaṇāni sādhakasya sādhanāni', the traits of a sthitaprajña should become guiding stars to all the sādhakas.

12

Om Ātmasvarūpāya Namaḥ

Salutations to the one who is the nature of the Self.

Swami Shashvatananda

How is Gurudev the ātmasvarūpa? The *Guru-gītā* (20.1) ratifies that He who is the Guru is Śiva Himself, and the fact that Śiva Himself is the Guru is pointed out to us in all the Smṛtis. O Pārvatī! I declare unto Thee, with all the emphasis at my command, that there is no difference between the Guru and the Ātman (Self). (*Guru-gītā* 25.1)

Clearly, the enlivening Ātman within is Gurudev!

The *Dakṣiṇāmūrti Stotram* says, "Salutations to Lord Dakṣiṇāmūrti, though all-pervasive like space, appears as though divided as Īśvara, Guru, and Ātman" – just as (the one) space is seemingly divided as Asia, Europe, Africa, and so on.

Gurudev is named Chinmayananda, which means Consciousness-Bliss. Consciousness illumines everything we perceive, think, feel, and do, as well as all our thoughts, feelings, and experiences, and the absence of all these.

Gurudev said, "Whenever you need me, close your eyes and look into your heart, and I will be there!" That presence within that we call upon in distress, that embraces us in response, that holds us to discipline – that presence and illuminer is the screen upon which these experiences of saṁsāra play.

Gurudev urged us to go beyond our experience to the illuminer. This is the nature of our ātmā. He is ātmasvarūpa.

And each of His nāma endorses our ātmasvarūpa. As the all-pervading Self, He is the 'awarer' (in us), our awareness, the 'awared', and the process of aware-ing. He is the one that drives our sādhana, our progress.

Thus, He proved for us the words of the *Guru-gītā,* "The Guru is Brahman and none other than Brahman Itself." The declaration that 'Guru is Brahman' is rare. He is attainable with difficulty and by the grace of God particularly. Gurudev is that God, Guru, and grace!

Gurudev symbolizes the power of His Guru, Shri Tapovan Maharaj. The Guru, who had at first dissuaded Him from leaving the hills for the chaos of the plains, later granted permission and also the power to communicate with us. Thus, He roared, exhorting us to detach from our ego and attach to our ātmasvarūpa.

Gurudev is that Ātman that took the persona of Chinmayananda. That He is the substratum upon which we all play is evident when we consider how He began His letters with 'Blessed Self' and signed off with, 'Thy Own Self'. He is the subject and the object, and thus He is ever the nature of the all-encompassing Ātman, that loves like a parent, plays like a friend, comforts like a mother, caring quietly all along.

He 'just knew' how the pieces of life's puzzle would arrange themselves and guided so many devotees. These are not to be seen as miracles; Gurudev's guidance was for the larger journey, towards the path, for a seeker on the path. Yes, many seekers enhance their journey with charity, pilgrimages, and so on, but if one tunes oneself to Him, these very processes become an offering unto Him, the Ātman, by the ātmasvarūpa, for the Ātman.

Like Hanumān, may we say, "When I am in my svarūpa, I am Thyself, Gurudev!"

etadvai satyakāma paraṃ cāparaṃ
ca brahma yadoṅkāraḥ,
tasmādvidvānetenaivāyatanenaikataramanveti.

O Satyakama! The syllable Om is indeed the symbol of both the lower and the higher Brahman; the conditioned and the unconditioned, the finite and the infinite. Therefore, he who knows it by this means surely attains either of them.

~ *Praśnopaniṣad* 5.2

13

Om Ānglabhāṣāviduttamāya Namaḥ

Salutations to the embodiment of eloquence in English.

Swami Dheerananda

After India's independence in 1947, even though the British haf left India, India's fascination for the English language and culture remained. People were enamored by the English language and considered those who spoke the language educated and civilized. Even those among the educated class, who had respect and yearning for Bhāratīya culture, did not know the glory and significance of it. Emerging at the time to remove this veil of ignorance that prevailed in the country was our Gurudev Swami Chinmayananda – a mysterious, mighty man of inner perfection, beauty, and glory. He was a man who could speak eloquently about the magnificent Bhāratīya culture while unraveling and breaking the myths in a language that many admired and appreciated. Naturally, people rushed to listen to Him. Indeed, it was a Hindu Renaissance.

Swami Chinmayananda's genius is the resurrection of the age-old tradition of yajña into *Gītā* jñāna-yajña, delving into 'The Art of Man Making'! His mastery of the scriptures of Sanātana Dharma, proficiency in English, commanding voice, charming personality, infinite patience, love, and tireless energy were how He communicated, to the eager and confused Indians, the true essence of freedom and happiness.

He captured the hearts of seekers by introducing the laws

of causation, and His remarkable Body-Mind-Intellect (BMI) chart became the GPS for any new seeker trekking to Truth.

The Chinmaya Mission Pledge, dictated spontaneously by Him, has now become the universal prayer invoking the powers of the Divine. The power of Mother Durgā is invoked so we become "courageous and disciplined, ever ready to fight against all low tendencies and false values, within and without us." The power of Mother Lakṣmī is invoked, so "we live honestly the noble life of sacrifice and service, producing more than what we consume and giving more than what we take." The power of Mother Saraswatī is invoked "to keep us on the path of virtue, courage, and wisdom."

Listening to Swami Chinmayananda was ecstasy. He was eloquence incarnate. Goddess Saraswatī joyfully danced on His tongue. He was Vedānta's voice in English.

When a reporter asked Him, "Do you have anything else to tell me?" Gurudev said, "I have nothing to tell. Keep Quiet. The only spiritual truth is shut up and get out!" Then Gurudev added, "I am not insulting you. Shut up in your mind, not your mouth. The next thought need not come. Get out of this misconception that you are a body. You are something more than a body. You are the all-pervading eternal essence, the Self, the Consciousness, the life in you. The life in you is the life everywhere. Discover your identity with God. And that cannot be done until you shut up. Therefore, all I can tell you is, 'Shut up and get out'!"

He majestically walked the divine path of 'love all', thus fulfilling the motto He gave to Chinmaya Mission, "to give maximum happiness to the maximum number for the maximum time!"

14

Om Īśvarāya Namaḥ

Salutations to the one who is the supreme Lord.

Swami Viviktananda

In the *Guru-gītā*, the Guru is equated with the great Trinity – Brahma the Generator, Viṣṇu the Operator, and Maheśvara the Destructor – GOD – who in His different aspects carries out the process of creation, sustenance, and constructive destruction. The *Guru-gītā* also says that the Guru is param Brahma – the absolute Reality itself. This description may confuse a novice sādhaka. But when the sādhaka advances in his spiritual journey, he realizes the importance of the *Guru-gītā* affirmation. This truth is reiterated in this sacred name of Pūjya Gurudev, Swami Chinmayananda: īśvarāya namaḥ – Salutations unto the Lord! The sādhaka, in his enlightened vision, addresses and invokes the Guru as the Lord Himself.

Īśvara is one who rules the whole universe. Like Lord Kṛṣṇa, Pūjya Gurudev could rule over the hearts of millions who met Him through His teachings and messages, directly or indirectly. The spell of spirituality that He cast over them stayed with them, slowly and steadily influencing their thoughts, words, and actions. He shone as a brilliant star in the firmament of their hearts, diffusing the light of knowledge, illumining every dark nook and corner of their lives.

Īśvara attracts everyone and everything but is not attracted by anyone or anything. Pūjya Gurudev, through His jñāna-yajñas, succeeded in making spiritual unfoldment happen in the lives of many aspirants and helped them manifest their divinity. The aspirants flocked to these yajñaśālās, where they received the 'inner initiation' or ignition to divine life. Coming under His spell of spiritual unfoldment, both men and women were drawn to the master, just like the gopās and gopikās were drawn to Lord Kṛṣṇa!

Vedānta speaks about the innate identity of the jīva and Īśvara. There is a world of difference between the two, literally and externally. According to Vedānta, Īśvara (Lord) is māyātīta (above the veil of māyā), and the jīva is māyādhīna (under the spell of māyā). Therefore, while the jīva suffers umpteen limitations, Īśvara controls māyā and is beyond all limitations. We jīvas, enslaved by the sense organs and the mind, get infatuated and are helplessly drawn to the world of objects and the resultant sufferings. But Īśvara, by his ability to not come under the spell of māyā, is ever the master of all situations. And so was Pūjya Gurudev! Realizing the illusoriness of the world that honored, worshipped, criticized, and denounced Him, He remained unperturbed, never coming under the spell of any attraction or distraction caused by the world. He was a master of all situations, holding His head ever high above the mundane happenings, whether in the vast world in general or even in the world of Chinmaya Mission, which has multiple centers across the globe with multifaceted sacred and secular activities. Thus, He successfully ushered in a spiritual renaissance in this world, continuously serving it but ever-abiding in His Self-experience of absolute Bliss and Peace.

15

Om Udārahṛdayāya Namaḥ

Salutations to the large-hearted one.

Swami Sharanananda

There is a very famous and popular subhāṣitam:

ayaṁ nijaḥ paro veti gaṇanā laghu cetasām,
udāracaritānām tu vasudhaiva kuṭumbakam.

"People with narrow minds spend their entire lives creating divisions in the world. But the noble-hearted ones consider the whole universe as one family – vasudhaiva kuṭumbakam."

Pūjya Gurudev Swami Chinmayananda embraced this aspect of loving and respecting everyone equally and unconditionally, be it an adult or a child, and saw everyone as one family. His love and vision of unity resulted in programs such as the Bala Vihar and various study groups.

In ancient times, students pursuing the study of Vedānta and spiritual practices were pure-minded and had genuine vairāgya for mumukṣutva (dispassion for liberation). But most of us who come to pursue the Vedānta course at Sandeepany Sadhanalaya don't seem to have the traits of a steadfast sādhaka. Even to such sādhakas, Swami Chinmayananda would impart the sublime knowledge of the Upaniṣads and the *Bhagavad-gītā*. This quality of unconditionally teaching anyone who desires to study Vedānta shows Pūjya Gurudev's udāratā.

His respect for women gave rise to the Devi Groups in

Chinmaya Mission. His concern for the underprivileged manifested in one of the most satisfying projects called CORD (Chinmaya Organization for Rural Development).

Though serving in Chinmaya Mission as sevaks, Swāmins, or Brahmacārins, we, too, committed errors unknowingly from time to time. But Pūjya Gurudev forgave one and all, accepted us as His children, and encouraged each one of us to continue to grow in the path of Vedānta. Because of His large-heartedness, even now, after thirty years of Pūjya Gurudev's mahāsamādhī, devotees in Chinmaya Mission get the same love, encouragement, and guidance just by being present in the Mission, where He continues to guide us from within. We are all safe and secure in His embrace. Let us all march ahead fearlessly and confidently in our spiritual journey.

Recognition and appreciation of the virtue of large-heartedness of Pūjya Gurudev is no doubt a great beginning, but we need to imbibe this quality sincerely and honestly to realize the meaning of this virtue that He lived by. As devotees of Pūjya Gurudev, we must accept and appreciate other devotees as they are without any judgment, fear, or doubt. Those who will not fit into this model will automatically stay away. Remember! He is always with us! Jai Gurudev!t

"Fully abiding in the peace and perfection of the Higher, in tune with the chaos and confusions of the lower, a Guru bridges the daunting gap between the seemingly unattainable Wisdom and what appears to be a never ending cesspool of sorrow, thus becoming a befitting spokesman for the Creator Himself."
~ Swami Chinmayananda

16

Om Utsāhavardhakāya Namaḥ

Salutations to the one who inspires.

Swami Chidatmananda

The word utsāha has many meanings – enthusiasm, zeal, energy, strength, power, fortitude, courage, resolution, effort, endurance, perseverance, cheerfulness, joy, and happiness; it also means initiative, inclination, and determination.

Pūjya Gurudev Swami Chinmayananda was an embodiment of all these qualities. There was a natural and spontaneous flow of enthusiasm, energy, zeal, and joy at all times in Gurudev. Each glance, smile, and gesture of His reflected every one of these qualities. These were not due to external factors but because He recognized the oneness with His inner Self. The one who has these qualities alone can bestow them upon others.

Some of Pūjya Gurudev's courageous and dedicated actions include fighting fearlessly in India's freedom movement and His efforts to go to great lengths to impart the knowledge of Brahma-vidyā, the ultimate knowledge that helps free a sādhaka from the bondage of saṁsāra to everyone who approached Him.

The word vardhaka, too, has many meanings, including augment, educate, strengthen, elevate, and exhilarate.

Gurudev was progressive in His thinking. The timeless knowledge that He imparted continues to help anyone face and overcome life's hurdles and progress spiritually. Imparting spiritual values through His teachings has only strengthened and elevated people. Those who followed His teachings and practiced these values have become prosperous in life, where they attained inner and outer richness. One can feel the inner strength in His entire śiṣya-paramparā.

When one follows His teachings, there is simply no scope for manipulation, self-aggrandizement, craving for recognition, or compromise of values; one remains content and fulfilled. This kind of inner state is the reward one gets, which is incomparable to any other external achievement. External success becomes like a shadow and follows wherever one goes. And the person remains unmindful of such success and gives no room for arrogance or egotism. All fears and sense of dependency vanish, manifesting independence and fearlessness within. This is the state of true utsāha. And Gurudev enhances and establishes such a state in those who live up to His teachings. Such people of inner fullness can only add to the peace, progress, and happiness in society and transform the nations.

May He ever live in our hearts and fill us with ever-increasing utsāha!

"With the blessings of what you have gained through this Knowledge, light a flicker of enthusiasm, which can unfurl a Renaissance of selfless attitude and intelligent living amongst the masses thereby rewriting the very history of an entire nation, hurtling it towards a glory never before encountered."
~ Swami Chinmayananda

17

Om Ekasmai Namaḥ

Salutations to the Supreme One.

Swami Advayananda

The expression ekasmai is derived from the Sanskrit word ekam, meaning 'one'. Thus, 'om ekasmai namaḥ' translates to – Om, Salutations unto the One!

Pūjya Gurudev, Swami Chinmayananda is our inspiration, way, and the goal. 'Ekam' is expressive of the goal, the supreme Reality, that the seeker yearns for. Verily Pūjya Gurudev is that goal, hence the salutations unto Him as Ekam. The *Chāndogya-upaniṣad* (6.2.1) declares that the ultimate Reality is 'ekam eva advitīyam' – One alone, with no other. Śrī Ādi Śankarācārya delineates that 'ekam' (one) is employed to indicate that Reality is bereft of svagata-bheda (internal differences). For example, a tree has many parts – root, stem, branch, leaf, and so on – each one is different in its own way. Such internal differences are termed svagata-bheda. Ekam emphasizes the absence of all such internal differences. The Supreme is homogeneous, unbroken, and devoid of all differences within Itself.

'Eva' (alone), the next expression, asserts that the Supreme is 'alone', meaning there is no sajātīya-bheda either. Within a single category, 'tree', there are wide varieties of trees. For example, a mango tree is different from a coconut tree. The differences within a particular category are termed sajātīya-bheda, and 'eva' underscores such an absence. Indeed, there is nothing similar to It. The third and last expression, 'advitīyam' (with no other), highlights the fact that Reality is non-dual and free of vijātīya-bheda, meaning there is nothing other that is different from It. For example, a tree is different from animals, birds, human beings, and so on. This sort of inter-species difference is vijātīya-bheda. 'Advitīyam' highlights that Reality is devoid of anything dissimilar to It, too.

Brahman, the supreme Reality, is homogeneous (ekam), with nothing similar (eva) or dissimilar (advitīyam) to It. This Brahman is verily Pūjya Gurudev! The scriptures proclaim this very same idea of 'ekam' by employing the suffix 'mayaṭ' to certain expressions that indicate the Highest. Thus the expressions 'sanmaya', 'ānandamaya', and so on denote the Reality being ekam or one homogeneous whole. While 'Cit' is Consciousness, 'Cinmaya' indicates consciousness 'alone'. Isn't our Gurudev by name also Chinmaya? Ekam!

The same intent of the Absolute being Ekam is also expressed with the suffix 'ghana', as in sadghana, cidghana, prajñānaghana, and so on. Yājñavalkya teaches Maitreyī in *Bṛhadāraṇyaka-upaniṣad* (4.5.13):

> *"As a lump of salt has neither inside nor outside and is but a homogeneous mass of taste, even so, this Self, my dear, has neither inside nor outside and is but a homogeneous mass of Consciousness (prajñānaghana)."*

This is probably the finest elucidation of 'ekam' in the literature of the Upaniṣads.

Glorifying and saluting that very highest Reality, Lord Kṛṣṇa, manifesting as the Virāṭa-puruṣa, Arjuna exclaims, "There exists none who is equal to You; how can there be then another superior to You?!" (*Bhagavad-gītā* 11.43). This is but a forceful exegesis of 'ekam' through the words of Arjuna!

There is no difference whatsoever between the Reality and the Guru. Ekam is the supreme Reality. Ekam is Shri Gurudev. Om ekasmai namaḥ!

18

Om Omkāravide Namaḥ

Salutations to the knower of Om.

Swamini Shivapriyananda

Omkāra or Om is the sacred mantra, the sacred sound symbol that represents the absolute Reality – the Infinite, the Eternal, the immutable Support and Enlivener of the entire cosmos. At the same time, it also refers to the Truth that cannot be perceived by the senses but can be 'known' through the grace of the Śruti (scriptures) and the Guru.

Whenever someone asked Pūjya Gurudev, Swami Chinmayananda, about the meaning of Om, He would answer succinctly, "You continue your sādhana, and Om will shine out!" To students of Vedānta, He would declare: "I am not the pointed; I am the pointer."

However, the fact is that Pūjya Gurudev was the very embodiment of Om; His mere presence was the personification of the Truth; His mission, His vision, His teaching, nay, His entire life, was dedicated to guiding humanity to the Supreme.

Since it is practically impossible to express this in a short essay, I quote Pūjya Gurudev's letter to a devotee who requested the Master to give him an autobiography. In it, many questions, known and unknown, regarding Gurudev have been clarified. In addition, the inimitable style of the letter itself speaks volumes!

"Blessed Self, Om Namo Narayanaya! Salutations!

I cannot give you an 'autobiography' only because I have got more interesting and very useful work in hand. But here are some positive points which should satisfy you for the time being. Later, I am sure you will try to shift your attention from me to the rishis and make your life beautiful and sublime.

I was born in Kerala, raised in the north, hardened in Punjab, softened in Uttarkashi, criticized everywhere, applauded in some places, but accepted and worshipped by everyone. I am a riddle to myself.

Prattling was my profession, preaching is my profession now, and I know that practice should be my future job. But everywhere, I earned a lot so far and squandered it all in the community. I am by training a religious man, by experience a Vedantin, by inclination a bhakta, in temperament a karma yogi, in practice an integral yogi. My faith is in democracy; I am convinced by socialism; I am habituated to communism; and I am committed to the impossible theory of "Love All".

Thick-skinned, hard-boned, I have an armor of laughter to cover and protect both my head and heart, so stabs do not penetrate me, spears cannot cleave me, and whippings do not lash me... You may meet me easily in my thirty-five books or in the puja room of any healthy young Indian, be they Hindu, Christian, or Muslim... My teacher was a divinely sweet, incandescent, noble soul, and I must tell you of Him when you grow a bit more. May I hope to hear from you often? Try. You can. Don't be shy. This is how everyone grows."

I am sure Gurudev's priceless words will serve as an invitation for a direct inquiry and help all sincere seekers in their spiritual journey and contemplation on Om.

19

Om Karuṇāsāgarāya Namaḥ

Salutations to the ocean of compassion.

Swami Abhedananda

The Consciousness conditioned by 'the desire to give liberation to the disciple' is called Guru! A Guru serves his disciple more than the disciple serves his Guru. A disciple can do puṣpāñjali archana of his Guru (offering of flowers), but the Guru does śabdāñjali archana to his disciple (offering of words), which alone sustains and nourishes the disciple's faith. When the disciple is under the refuge of the Guru, he receives a mother's love, a father's discipline, and a friend's companionship!

From the highest realms of meditation, the Guru comes down to the level of the disciple, and therefore, it requires a heart filled with immense compassion, patience, and utmost forgiveness. Such was the heart of our Pūjya Gurudev Swami Chinmayananda. The more we realize, think, contemplate, and get colored with the benign nature of Pūjya Gurudev, the more our heart gets overwhelmed with devotion and surrender unto Him. He truly epitomizes the name 'om karuṇāsāgarāya namaḥ' – the infinite ocean of compassion!

There is a touching and memorable incident that happened in my life in the year 1991, which reminds me of the oceanic compassion of Gurudev. As a young boy just out of college, I was very excited to attend Pūjya Gurudev's Suvarṇa Tulābhāra event. Despite all my efforts, I was late, and when I reached the venue, the tulābhāra had ended. I was sad and asked the Lord why I was not blessed to witness that golden moment. But then I thought maybe the Lord had other plans for me and that I shouldn't lose heart. So I rushed to the Chinmaya Mission Powai āśram. Right outside Gurudev's cottage, many people were waiting for Him. I stood in a corner amidst the crowd when I saw Pūjya Gurudev entering in a wheelchair. One glance at me, and He exclaimed with joy, "Ah! You have come!" I was stunned and couldn't believe my eyes or ears. He called me again, "I am talking to you. Come here." I walked towards Him, and to my sheer disbelief and inexplicable joy, He held my hands tightly, addressed me by my name, and asked, "Where were you? I was looking for you and waiting for you. So good you have come. Now, are you happy?" I was speechless, moved, and couldn't say a word. That moment of Him holding my hands while looking into my eyes, saying He was waiting for me, makes me feel like He still is holding my hands and will never leave me!

Our Gurudev was not a vyaṣṭi puruṣa (microcosmic person), He was a samaṣṭi puruṣa (macrocosmic person). He was not just one member of humanity; He was an institution! Gurudev was not just a Guru to His disciples, but a walking, talking God; He was the very manifestation of the *Gītā* and Upaniṣads. He did not just give discourses, but rather the *Gītā* and Upaniṣads expressed through Him!

The more we surrender our ego and attachment to Pūjya Gurudev, the more intense His compassion will engulf us. Fortunate are we who got the opportunity to bask in His love and continue to bathe in the infinite Ganga of Chinmaya Mission, which is the karuṇā mūrti (symbol of compassion) of Pūjya Gurudev. Let us merge our smallness in Him so that we cease to exist, and only Him and His glory are seen all around! My infinite prostrations to this great Mahātmā of the era!

20

Om Karmaparāyaṇāya Namaḥ

Salutations to the one engaged in action.

Swamini Umananda

All the names in Śrī Chinmaya Aṣṭottara Śata Nāmāvali describe the glory of our beloved Gurudev. Either they describe the characteristics of the Realized Master that He was, or they describe the divine qualities that are common to all great masters, or they glorify the divine Self through His specific form. Meditating on these three aspects embodied by Gurudev through His names is a channel of great inspiration.

As said in the *Bhagavad-gītā*, everybody has to engage in action – even a Realized Master. As long as we are alive, we will act physically, mentally, or intellectually. But, of course, there is a significant difference between the action of a Liberated Master and the action of a person still in the clutches of the ego. In a saint, the action springs from Knowledge; in an egoistic person, the action is born from ignorance. The word 'Knowledge' here indicates the highest viveka: a clear understanding of the real doer.

One of the big questions that Vedānta raises is: "Who really acts? Who is the doer? Is it the ego?" No, because this limited and illusory subject does not control anything. Of course, the individual must be there, but he is not the real doer. Is the Self the real doer? No, because Its nature is immutable It is pure Existence-Consciousness. So, who is the doer? Any action is possible only because of the divine Energy (Śakti) emanating from the Self and enlivening all the instruments of experience. Through this Energy, the actions are made at the levels of the instruments of experience and are seen by the Witness, the Self. When this Knowledge is attained, the action becomes right, beneficial, and divine. Gurudev was an embodiment of this Knowledge. He acted with total inner freedom and consecration to the Lord, with total detachment, using His body-mind-intellect to do what had to be done in the service of the Lord. As said in the *Bhagavad-gītā*, He acted "without attachment, for the benefit of the world."

His exemplary life of service and His teachings remain ever-present to guide us. Gurudev insisted on the transformative power of a spiritualized action (karma yoga). If we act without being centered on our selfish desires but turn to a higher goal, motivated by pure love, slowly, the tyranny of the ego is reduced. Gradually, we will reach the beautiful step of surrender, where it is neither our will nor desire for control that counts but only the will of the Lord. From this stage of surrender, the ultimate goal can be attained one day, realizing the Self as our true nature.

In June 1993, Gurudev came to Paris to give a talk. We were doing the final round of preparations for the evening program. Swamiji, who was resting in His room, came out and sat with us, watching the preparations. We were making badges that the team members would wear in the evening with an 'Om' drawn on an orange background. He looked at one carefully and said, "Well done! With this, people will know that you are ready to serve..." As taught by Gurudev, let us act with love and a spirit of service – To be always ready to serve. What a beautiful instruction!

21

Om Kālātītāya Namaḥ

Salutations to the one who is beyond time.

Swami Chidrupananda

To understand the meaning of kālātīta, we need to know what time is, its definition, and how Gurudev had mastered it. Time is defined as an interval between two events. However, there is another definition – krama saṃvit kālaḥ – the awareness of the sequence of events is time. Unless there is awareness illumining the events, there is no time at all. Since there is no awareness in deep sleep, there is no time there as well.

Time is born only when there is a movement. If there is no movement, there is no time. Physical time is due to the movements of the sun and the planets. Psychological time is born of the thoughts (they too, change or move). Psychological time is subjective, whereas physical time is common to all. If I like a lecture, time flies, otherwise not. Therefore, a movement plus awareness of the movement creates time.

Pūjya Gurudev said that the unit of time is 'second' and not 'first' because, at the first event, time is not born. Only at the end of the second event one unit of time is born. Therefore, the unit of time is called 'second' and not 'first'.

Gurudev is kālātīta – the one who is beyond time. He utilized time intelligently in many ways.

Whenever Gurudev made a saṅkalpa, everything tended to fall into place to make it happen. As an example, when we look at Gurudev's itinerary, we would notice that there were rarely any changes that were made once His itinerary was set. Time cooperated non-stop for forty-two years with Gurudev.

Another quality of the one who has mastered time is that the person never gets tired. Gurudev never exhibited physical fatigue, except due to illness at times. When someone asked about His health, He replied, "Shhh! Don't ask loudly. The body doesn't know that it is sick."

Gurudev never felt the stress of His never-ending work. Even with the body subjected to changes and facing health challenges, Gurudev was never mentally stressed. His non-stop work for forty-two years is the proof that is in front of all of us. We never heard Gurudev say, "I am under stress; I cannot handle work." Gurudev knew the nature of time, and therefore, His planning was always perfect, considering seasons, place, and the kind of listeners. He used time intelligently, and time had to obey His commands.

Once we had planned a question-and-answer session with Pūjya Gurudev for the youth in Hyderabad. Over 1000 youth and around 200 adults attended the session, but given Gurudev's health, He could not participate fully. When we told Gurudev that we would like to restrict the questions to about eight or nine, Gurudev looked at me and said – "No! Let them ask as many as they want. Collect the questions with their addresses. I will write to them all." I was awestruck when around thirty of them received letters with a sentence on the top right side of the letter – "In flight to Mumbai from Hyderabad." He never rested, even during His travels.

Gurudev ruled time and utilized it for service, for He had transcended time and identified Himself with the eternal all-pervading spirit. This is the key to His mastery of time. To such a great Master who is beyond time, my salutations!

22

Om Kaivalyasvarūpāya Namaḥ

Salutations to the one whose nature is Absolute Oneness.

Swamini Kaivalyananda

In May 1989, a special Viṣnusahasranāma archana was organized to celebrate Pūjya Gurudev's seventy-third birthday. Innumerable birthday greetings poured in, but Pūjya Gurudev's message was, "The celebrations are for you all. This body doesn't belong to me. I am Unborn, the Self in every one of you."

It is difficult for a teacher who has experienced Consciousness, the highest Self, where there is no duality, to teach students who are on the empirical plane. Pūjya Gurudev was one of the few Masters who tirelessly and at ease taught all through His life whether one deserved that knowledge or not.

During one of my short trips with Pūjya Gurudev, I met a devotee, Sakuntala Bindra in Delhi, who attended Gurudev's *Māṇḍūkya-upaniṣad* yajña in 1953. Her experience during the yajña made me reflect a lot. She said, "Pūjya Gurudev was brimming with joy all through the yajña in that highest state of experience, and we could not understand His subtle teachings then. By the time we understood, He became very busy."

As I was archiving the glories of Pūjya Gurudev, I chanced upon His first yajña prasād, where Gurudev had written, "Chinmaya's work is dedicated to the Śrutis which speak of what reality is, Shri Tapovan Maharaj who guided me to the end and pushed me into the beyond, and to Shri Sivananda Maharaj who showed me in his life how to live and act in God as God." A Master of that highest caliber rarely talked about Himself but wanted every one of us to experience that kaivalya state. Nonstop for decades, He gave us that knowledge and wanted His disciples to experience what He had experienced from His Masters.

After completing the Vedānta course, I met Gurudev for the last time in 1993 with an agitated mind, wondering whether He had accepted me as His disciple. During a satsaṅg later, He looked at me directly, answering my question, and said, "Anybody who has any doubt about whether I have accepted them as my disciple should do guru upāsanā." After some moments of silence, He roared, "Turn within. This is the only method by which you can get out of this mad world!" This was the message Gurudev gave all of us. He promised to wait for us until we experience that oneness with Him.

Once, I read a letter from Gurudev, written in the early fifties, to an old devotee where He encouraged her to ask more questions, "Shoot! Don't spare the Swami till the last doubt is cleared from your bosom. Shoot! Don't spare the Swami till His muscles are dissolved, and the last drop of blood is drained. Make use of your Swami as much as you can." I became very emotional on reading the letter. Until the last breath, Pūjya Gurudev served unconditionally so we could experience the kaivalya sthiti that He had experienced.

I'm like a mere firefly trying to describe the glories of Gurudev, whose presence was sheer brilliance like the mighty Sun. May we not fall short in our sādhana to give our best to experience that ultimate state, the knowledge our Gurudev has given us so selflessly.

23

Om Kṛtātmane Namaḥ

Salutations to the self-made one.

Swami Shuddhananda

One who has mastery over their body, mind, and intellect is a kṛtātma. Whenever we chant the nāma 'om kṛtātmane namaḥ', we are paying our respects to Pūjya Gurudev's commitment, hard work, extraordinary knowledge of the scriptures, and dedication towards vedik culture. Pūjya Gurudev has done tremendous work for Hinduism by spreading the knowledge of the *Gītā* and the Upaniṣads. This is not possible until one has mastery over their body, mind, and intellect.

Everybody has a turning point in their life. I feel that this turning point came in Pūjya Gurudev's life when He met Swami Sivananda Maharaj, founder of The Divine Life Society, in Rishikesh in 1949. The second important turning point in the life of Pūjya Gurudev was the life events that followed soon after He took sannyāsa dīkṣā in the year 1949. He was asked by his dīkṣā Guru, Swami Sivananda Maharaj, to go to Uttarkashi and study the śāstras under the guidance of Swami Tapovan Maharaj. As we know, Gurudev had not brought an introductory letter written by Swami Sivananda to Swami Tapovan Maharaj. So Swami Tapovan Maharaj sent Gurudev back and told him to come back with a letter. This happened in the year 1949, about seventy-five years ago when there was no transportation, proper roads, or other facilities. But Gurudev showed His commitment. Gurudev traveled the difficult terrain of 165 kilometers from Rishikesh to Uttarkashi, climbing hills and crossing rivers, not once but twice, on foot.

After the formation of Chinmaya Mission in 1953, He traveled extensively in India and abroad to spread the message of the *Gītā* and the Upaniṣads. Even when He was not physically fit, He conducted classes showing His mastery over the body and mind. What to say about Him intellectually! That is why He is called a kṛtātma.

Another meaning of kṛtātma is the one who revels in Brahman even while performing welfare activities for others. Pūjya Gurudev started Chinmaya Mission for people to study religion and philosophy in a systematic manner under the gurukula system, where the students lived with the Guru for the period of their education. During His first jñāna-yajña in Pune, Gurudev single-handedly managed everything, right from the announcements to the discourses, despite people raising objections to giving the knowledge of the *Gītā* and Upaniṣads to common people, and that too in English. But Pūjya Gurudev always had a plan of action. From 1953 to 1993, till His mahāsamādhī, He did remarkable and extraordinary work in every field, right from conducting more than one thousand jñāna yajñas to starting schools, building homes for the elderly, āśrams, and so on.

I live in Port Blair, Andaman and Nicobar Islands. Gurudev visited these Islands for the first time in 1980 when there was only one flight operating to the Islands. But Gurudev thought of starting a Chinmaya Mission center in these Islands, because of His commitment to making people spiritually strong even in far-flung places like Andamans.

I offer my sincere praṇāms and salutations to the holy feet of a great visionary, a dynamic spiritual mentor, a patriotic saint, a disciplined master, and above all, a kind-hearted, extraordinary human being!

24

Om Kṛtakṛtyāya Namaḥ

Salutations to the content one.

Swami Sharadananda

Pūjya Gurudev, Swami Chinmayananda, dedicated His life to rejuvenate the ancient wisdom of Sanātana Dharma. He had attained Bliss and complete fulfillment (kṛtakṛtyatā) in life. The word kṛtakṛtya appears in *Bhagavad-gītā* (15.20). Śrī Ādi Śankarācārya, in his commentary, interprets kṛtakṛtya as "one who has fulfilled all that needs to be accomplished." *Bhagavad-gītā* proclaims, "Fulfillment of all actions is only with the attainment of Self-Knowledge." (4.33)

Gurudev's vision for a better society transformed Him into a kṛtakṛtya under the tutelage of His Gurus, Swami Sivananda Maharaj and Tapovan Maharaj. His kṛtakṛtyatā encompassed various facets of human existence.

In the transactional realm, individuals perform actions with the notion of 'I am the doer' with an expectation of results. However, a kṛtakṛtya like Pūjya Gurudev does tremendous, selfless work transcending personal desires. How so? *Avadhūtopaniṣad* (26) states: "Even though I have attained what must be achieved, let me persist on the path of scripture for the betterment of the world." *Bhagavad-gītā* (3.20) states, "Considering the welfare of the people, you ought to act."

Gurudev exemplifies this commitment, leaving behind a contemplative Himalayan life for a mission to awaken the masses despite His Guru's initial discouragement. As a jñānī, rooted in perceiving oneness, Gurudev, in His kṛtakṛtyatā, served humanity without seeking any gain as He wanted us to experience the same blissful state of completeness.

As a kṛtakṛtya, Gurudev had complete emotional equilibrium (samatva) due to His identification with His true nature of eternal Bliss. He inspired others to overcome emotional bondages (cravings and aversions) by advocating willpower or channeling them towards God as devotion. Gurudev's boundless grace brought solace to countless devotees, nurturing their emotional well-being and overall welfare through personal interactions and correspondence.

Gurudev attained the intellectual fulfillment of kṛtakṛtyatā, by not just being a jñānī (knower) but a vijñānī (experiencer) of the true Self. Through jñāna-yajñas, Gurudev sparked an intellectual awakening among the masses, addressing inquisitive and agnostic minds with innovative tools like the Body-Mind-Intellect Chart and postal Vedānta courses, making Vedānta accessible to all while preserving its essence. Authoring commentaries on Upaniṣads, *Bhagavad-gītā*, and other Vedānta and bhakti texts, He stressed on intellectual discipline rooted in ancient wisdom.

In the spiritual realm, Gurudev's kṛtakṛtyatā manifested as a jīvanmukta (one liberated in life) with complete abidance in the Self. He was both śrotriya (versed in scriptures) and brahmaniṣṭha (rooted in the Self) traversing diverse paths to the Supreme and opening the gates of evolution for others to realize their true nature.

Gurudev's work in individual transformation encompassed the betterment of society as a whole, and His legacy remains an enduring source of inspiration and guidance. Pūjya Gurudev, as kṛtakṛtya, ensured that future generations could also find the same fulfillment by treading the path shown by śāstras and Mahātmās. May Gurudev bless all of us with kṛtakṛtyatā in all aspects of life.

triṣu dhāmasu yadbhogyaṁ bhoktā
bhogaśca yadbhavet,
tebhyo vilakṣaṇaḥ sākṣī
cinmātro'haṁ sadāśivaḥ.

All that constitute the enjoyable, the enjoyer and the enjoyment in the three realms – different from them all am I, the Witness, the Ever-Auspicious, pure Consciousness.

~ *Kaivalyopaniṣad* 18

25

Om Gītā-jñāna-yajña-pracārakāya Namaḥ

Salutations to the propagator of the knowledge of the Bhagavad-gītā.

Swamini Radhikananda

While still in Uttarkashi, learning the teachings of Vedānta everyday, at the feet of the Shri Swami Tapovan Maharaj, the great Master himself once told Gurudev, “Go sit by the Ganga. She alone can teach you.” After years of great physical austerity, service to His Guru, and intense study and meditation, Gurudev Himself later described how, one day, as He sat by the Ganga river, He seemed to hear her voice calling to Him: “Son, don’t you see me? Born here in the Himalayas, I rush down to the plains, taking with me both life and nourishment to all in my path. Fulfillment of any possession is in sharing it with others!”

Following a year of travel on foot around India and finally receiving Tapovan Maharaj’s blessings for His inspired endeavor, Pūjya Gurudev’s stupendous ‘Gangotri Plan’ of sharing the life-transforming teachings of the *Bhagavad-gītā* in English began; first as a trickle, then quickly flooding the entire world as He traveled without rest for over forty years!

Gurudev’s immense tapas and compassion drew down the flowing grace of knowledge to this world when we needed it most, reinterpreted for our modern understanding. It was Gurudev’s boundless, unconditional love alone, that made

Him descend the mountain to look for us in whatever country or culture we came from, to gather us together and to light the yajña-fire that would consume our delusion and sorrow and give us spiritual rebirth in the waters of eternal Truth. His *Gītā* song became the sweet, soul-enchanting melody of Śrī Kṛṣṇa's flute echoing through the forest of our hearts, beckoning us, with laughter and joy, to join Him in the Lord's rāsa-līlā of divine love and bliss, the dance of Realization!

Among innumerable personal memories, one stands out with unforgettable impact, when, on the first night of one such yajña in Mumbai, we, Sandeepany students at the time, had been on an hour's kīrtan-procession around several city blocks as an announcement for the event. We were returning to the yajña site when Gurudev suddenly appeared in front of us. Our hearts and voices lifted in exaltation, and the brahmacārīs began dancing spontaneously in ecstasy around Gurudev as He strode towards the gates of the yajña grounds! Upon entering, Gurudev walked alone with quick, majestic, and single-pointed stride towards the stage to deliver His divine message. How exceedingly blessed we were to be among the thousands and millions of souls who heard Him in the *Gītā* jñāna-yajña halls, spellbound by His words and powerful presence!

Shri Tapovan Maharaj gave Him the jñāna. Mother Ganga gave Him His calling. He became the song of the *Gītā* and spent His life's breath singing so that we, too, might hear and sing with Him and become the song. Can you hear it? May Gurudev give us the grace to answer His call.

26

Om Gurave Namaḥ

Salutations to the perceptor.

Swami Mitrananda

Gurudev always used every opportunity to impart the knowledge of the sublime truths. Once we accompanied Him to the railway station. As we stood on the platform, a goods train passed by. "Look through the gap between the coaches to see the other side. In the same way, in the seat of meditation, practice looking through the gap between the thoughts." A simple incident, like a train passing by, becomes a beautiful lesson in the art of meditation. Generally, the thought current is so strong that we get carried away by it. But by diligent practice, one can master this skill of observing the gap when one thought ends and the other begins. Any small incident, Gurudev would creatively employ to help us turn our minds to the Higher. He did not always need the book or the formal lecture to inspire the students. A genuine teacher dedicates every moment of his life for the sake of the students.

Once, an army officer who was accompanying Gurudev for the evening talks explained to Him the value the uniform has for the army men. He told how army officers are expected to maintain a sense of discipline and decorum when in uniform. On hearing this, Swamiji quipped back, "My Guru gave me a uniform, and I am expected to wear it even while sleeping." One cannot be a part-time sannyāsin. A seeker is a seeker all through his life. And the pursuit of the higher becomes the topmost priority in his life.

Gurudev lived the life of a teacher, 24×7, 365 days a year. He was not a teacher only during the talks. One of His disciples remarked once, "With Him, every breath was a teaching." There is a Zen quote that says, "In a dark room, where no one else is present, a wise man conducts himself as if in the presence of a noble guest." It is important to express spontaneously one's inherent nature. A genuine human being cannot have dual personalities – one when he is alone and one when being observed by others. As a teacher, one has to be conscious that he is being observed by his students always, and not just in the classroom. Elders, especially school teachers, should remember that students always look up to their teachers, whether in or outside the classroom. The responsibilities of a teacher do not end with the class. So it is important that all the elders, especially teachers, live the values they cherish always. Because at any given moment, someone might be watching and emulating them.

My salutations to Him, who dedicated each and every moment to nurturing and mentoring the eager students.

"In the presence of the Guru, the mind automatically surrenders to the Divine, experiencing blissful awareness. We strive for such moments of hushed silence in our meditation sessions and try to reach those moments again and again. But in the Guru's presence, the silence envelops us without even striving for it. What takes us months during sadhana, a Guru can accomplish it in a moment."
~ Anjali Singh

27

Om Guṇātītāya Namaḥ

Salutations to the one who is beyond all attributes.

Swami Prakarshananda

Human birth is indeed rare, but rarer is an individual's desire for liberation (mokṣa icchā), the yearning for liberation (mumukṣutvam). According to the scriptures, this is the result of merits accumulated from thousands of past lives. Every sincere seeker with an honest and single-pointed desire for a spiritual life will surely reach a competent Guru and experience the highest state indicated by the scriptures. In the *Bhagavad-gītā* (14.25), Bhagavān describes a Realized Master as guṇātīta (one who has crossed over all guṇas) – the one who is the same in honor and dishonor, is the same to friend and foe, and has abandoned all egocentric desire-ridden actions."

A Realized Master like our Pūjya Gurudev Swami Chinmayananda was free of all identification with the body, mind, and intellect (BMI). Pūjya Gurudev came to this earth to redeem us and lift us all from our state of ignorance.

The universe is extremely colorful, but its nature is ever-changing; its names and forms are superimposed on the Self. Amongst the flimsy objects of the world, the mind influenced by the three guṇas (sattva, rajas, and tamas) gets completely carried away. Magically powerful, these guṇas can even hide the Truth and project the unreal as real. Some rare daredevils are blessed with the courage to leap across the thick boundaries of triguṇātmikā māyā (*Kaṭhopaniṣad* 2.1.1).

"The Self-existent Lord created the outgoing senses. Therefore, one sees outer things and not the inner Self. A rare discriminating person, desiring immortality, turns his attention within to discover and revel in the indwelling Self."

On the path of knowledge, the eligibility of a seeker is an essential factor. The essence of sādhana-catuṣṭaya, the fourfold qualifications for a seeker, highlights the need to develop total dispassion towards everything in life, including the body, mind, and intellect. In the *Bhagavad-gītā* (2.45), Śrī Kṛṣṇa, through Arjuna, clearly indicates the importance of developing these qualities of the heart to those whose end goal is to get established in the Self and rise into the state of triguṇātītāvasthā.

- nistraiguṇyo bhava – become desireless – The Lord strictly directs us to give up all ego-centric desires
- nirdvandvo bhava – free from all pairs of duality
- nitya sattvastho bhava – remain poised and unwavering in goodness (sattva)
- niryogakṣema – devoid of desires for acquisition and preservation
- ātmavān – whose mind is only focused on the Self

These guṇas cannot be destroyed. The seeker ultimately rises beyond their influence by getting established in pure sattva (śuddhasattva) by realizing the Self.

Gurudev lived in a state of absolute detachment, above the influence of three guṇas, with zero identification with the world around Him. There was no doer-ship or enjoyer-ship. He enjoyed the state of Absolute Freedom. He was beyond the identification with the three guṇas – guṇātīta.

28

Om Granthakṛte Namaḥ

Salutations to the author of scriptural texts.

Swami Avyayananda

The word 'granthakṛt' – is made up of two parts. The first part, 'grantha', can mean:

- to arrange in a sequence or order
- to write, create, or compose
- a sacred text

The second part 'kṛt' can mean: to make or to do; or 'kṛnt': to destroy.

Combining the meanings of these two, let us explore the qualities of our Pūjya Gurudev hidden in this sacred name.

Pūjya Gurudev served society at various levels leading every individual towards the knowledge of the scriptures. Gurudev's talks contained thoughts and concepts logically arranged and interspersed with relevant examples, which enabled even mediocre students to grasp the subtle messages. Besides, Gurudev also had a very systematic way of doing things that He taught all of us. The manuals for various grassroots activities like Bala Vihar, Chinmaya Yuva Kendra, study groups, and so on are testimony to this.

In Vedānta, creation is explained to be a sequence of events, at the root of which is māyā – the primordial power of Brahman. This māyā or ignorance, which brings about a sequential creation, that is, space, air, fire, water, earth, and so on, is destroyed by gaining knowledge of Brahman. Pūjya Gurudev spent over four decades spreading this knowledge across the world, thereby destroying ignorance from the hearts and lives of seekers.

Pūjya Gurudev built several āśramas, temples, centers, schools, and other institutions to serve humanity. His out-of-the-box thinking and brilliant creativity were experienced by all those who came in touch with Him in various ways. Who else but Pūjya Gurudev could write about a hundred letters every day! Thousands of devotees have been blessed recipients of these love and guidance-filled letters.

The greatest enemy of a creative person is the sense of doer-ship – becoming the 'creator' and getting attached to our little creation. Pūjya Gurudev created this grand global organization, Chinmaya Mission, but neither took credit for it nor was He attached to it. When asked about the future of the Chinmaya Mission, Gurudev humbly said, "This (Chinmaya Mission) has come from Nārāyaṇā and will remain as long as He wills." On various occasions, Gurudev also ensured the destruction of such ego in devotees and disciples.

Chinmaya Mission has a huge wealth of precious books ranging from stories for children to thought-provoking articles for the youth and lucid explanations of scriptural concepts for all seekers. These books written by Pūjya Gurudev are a great source of inspiration and guidance to the young and old even today and will remain so forever.

The realized Master, our Pūjya Gurudev, was beyond the scriptures and often guided all seekers to use the words of the scriptures just as a pole-vaulter used the pole. Another example that Pūjya Gurudev used to give in this regard is that of a milestone and destination – the pointer and the Pointed!

He is the Pointed, our Goal! To such a great Master, we are ever indebted.

29

Om Cinmayāya Namaḥ

Salutations to the one who is pure Consciousness.

Swami Turiyananda

In Sanskrit, 'Cit' (chit) means consciousness or that which knows. Cit + mayam = Cinmayam, that which is made up of Cit; that which is the abode of knowledge.

Pūjya Gurudev Swami Chinmayananda, true to His name, was an embodiment of knowledge of the Self. He was indeed a sage who realized the Self and lived His entire life to teach Self-knowledge to seekers. Inspired by the holy Ganga, He took the knowledge of Vedānta to the masses so that it could dispel the ignorance that causes all sufferings in our day-to-day lives.

For more than forty-two years of His lifetime, every day, somewhere in the world, He would be teaching the knowledge of the *Bhagavad-gītā* or the Upaniṣads or any of the topics related to Vedānta. He not only taught Vedānta but also lived that knowledge and showed to the world that Vedānta is not just a mere intellectual theory but can be practiced in daily life.

Whatever work that Pūjya Gurudev would take up, He would do with full awareness, be it writing a simple letter, folding an envelope, or addressing thousands of devotees at a jñāna-yajña. It was indeed a lesson to all of us to live in the present with awareness instead of brooding over the past or being anxious about the future. He was always at the highest level of consciousness, and He would advise devotees to meet Him in the seat of meditation.

A lamp that is lit alone can light other lamps. He established Sandeepany Sadhanalaya to impart this ancient wisdom of our great ṛṣis to future generations. He spread the knowledge of our ancient scriptures to thousands of people in various countries in the world through Chinmaya Mission, just as a lamp spreads its light in all directions. He simplified this knowledge with His own style of expounding and brought this to everybody's life in society, right from children to senior citizens.

Namaḥ (salutation) is indicative of devotion. *Nārada Bhakti Sūtra* (2) says:

sā tu asmin paramaprema rūpā

"Devotion is supreme love where you become one with the Lord or Guru."

So, when we worship Pūjya Gurudev with the mantra, 'om cinmayāya namaḥ', we should identify ourselves with Pūjya Gurudev as the Self, identify with His vision of transforming individuals with the knowledge of Vedānta, and identify with His Mission of selfless service to humanity.

"Hundreds of thousands of people delighted to hear Swamiji's Vedanta talks. People saw His amazing presence and heard a force of inspiring dynamism, an energy that swept into one's heart and opened it to greater wisdom. But one strong quality of Swamiji's was not so apparent on stage – his deep, penetrating, soul-stirring silence. Swamiji taught this silence off-stage. It is this teaching that made him a living Upaniṣad. In this silence, the mind gets hushed, and the joy lying within one's being comes forth. Swamiji was always in this silence."
~ Vilasini Balakrishnan

30

Om Cinnasaṁśayāya Namaḥ

Salutations to the one who dispels doubts.

Swami Swatmananda

Vedānta challenges our most fundamental ideas. It says we are not the body, mind, and intellect; the creation is unreal or illusory; the supreme Reality alone exists, and it is our true nature. This naturally creates many doubts in our minds.

When we listen (śravaṇam) to our scriptures, especially the mahāvākyas from a Sadguru, if our mind is ready, we realize instantly. If it's not yet pure and subtle, doubts will arise. With faith in the scriptures, using scriptural logic when we do our reflection (mananam) and discuss with co-seekers, we develop an intellectual conviction. This alone is not enough to dispel the doubts. There is a habitual error of false identification with the body-mind-intellect, which does not allow us to experience the Self. Pūjya Gurudev said, "Doubts are but the shadows of your own mind's dancing. Quieten the mind through meditation, study, and realize That which is beyond all doubts." Habitual error is removed by contemplation (nididhyāsanam) and we come to discover the Truth. We see this in the life of Pūjya Gurudev.

When a young agnostic Balan met Swami Sivananda, questioned him, and observed his selfless life of service, he transformed into a believer and even went on to take sannyāsa and became Swami Chinmayananda. Yet he had many more questions. Swami Sivananda sent him to Swami Tapovanam of Uttarkashi to study Vedānta systematically.

Swami Tapovanam would teach only once, and when he asked any questions, if Swami Chinmayananda was not able to answer, he would have to leave. Swamiji agreed. In turn, Swamiji would ask many questions and would not allow Him to move on to the next topic until every doubt was cleared. This way, Swamiji studied *Pañcadaśi* and a few Upaniṣads. He would listen to the lectures in Hindi and write his notes in English. He would spend hours after each lesson, making sure that no thought was incomplete, no insight undigested. He contemplated upon it intensely. Swamiji followed the sādhana of śravaṇam, mananam, nididhyāsanam, and savikalpa and nirvikalpa samādhi to awaken to the supreme Truth. *Muṇḍaka-upaniṣad* (2.2.8) says, "When It (Truth) is seen both in the higher and the lower, the knot of his heart becomes untied, all doubts are dispelled, and all his karmas are consumed."

Pūjya Gurudev's love for the students, selflessness to share knowledge, and zeal to revive Sanātana Dharma enabled Him to empathize with the questioners and answer them at their level.

A youngster in Chennai asked Pūjya Gurudev, "What is a vāsanā?" His reply was, "When a young girl is walking on the road, the tendency in you that makes you want to whistle is called a vāsanā." He did not use technical terms like unmanifest, cause of gross and subtle body, and so on. He spoke in a language that the youth would understand.

He spoke from the standpoint of non-believers, which convinced them as well as the believers. Many devotees felt that even without asking their doubts would be cleared in the talk. Great Masters do not even have to speak, their presence is enough.

31

Om Jagadātmane Namaḥ

Salutations to the one for whom the world is the Self.

Vilasini Balakrishnan

Gurudev Swami Chinmayananda was recovering from His triple bypass heart surgery in August 1980. Post-surgery, Gurudev spent about six weeks in the United States on strict rest. He was very frail at the beginning and doctors required that someone be with Him at all times, even at night, in case of emergencies.

Several doctors managed His care and travel. Gurudev also appointed Nalini Browning and Vilasini Balakrishnan to travel with Him while recuperating. Even though there were no public gatherings or satsaṅgs, there were still people always around Him. Before this, Gurudev used to have some quietude during His afternoon rest and at night, but now there was always someone with Him! Observing this constant company, one morning, Nalini asked Gurudev, "Swamiji, with all of us around all the time, don't you ever get tired of us?" Gurudev looked at her sternly and said softly, "You may get tired of wearing the same clothes day after day, but do you ever get tired of your arms and legs?!" We looked incredulously at each other, realizing that Gurudev truly saw us as part of Himself. Despite His weakened state, He felt His devotees were a part of Him.

Gurudev loved those around Him so much. We used to wonder how He could love us all so deeply, when we were filled with vāsanās and human frailties. He could see the divine potential in each of us and would lovingly try to coax our highest potential out of us. He could read our thoughts and knew our motives. He could speak to each person in an audience of thousands, and each one would say at the end of the talk, "Swamiji was speaking to me alone in that discourse. He read my mind and answered my doubts."

This siddhi of knowing all our thoughts, doubts, and aspirations is possible only for a Jagadguru, one who sees Himself in others and others in Himself.

Jagad-Ātman is a beautiful name for our Gurudev. It can be parsed in a few ways, all of which apply to Him. Jagad-Ātman: The Self of the world, or the One who sees the world as Himself. *Īśāvāsya-upaniṣad* states this truth in its opening mantra: "This entire universe is indwelt and pervaded by Īśā, the Lord." Gurudev writes in His commentary: "The world-of-matter acts as the veil, covering from our vision the Divinity within, and therefore we are unable to perceive the Divine Presence everywhere around us. Bring out the Lord to envelop the phenomenal world, and thus, in His Infinite Light, let the experience of multiplicity be to the enlightened seeker a vision clothed in celestial Light Divine."

We, who were touched by Gurudev's grace, either in person or by His spirit, know that He indeed saw the whole world and all of us in it as bathed in the Divine Light and Spirit, and spent His lifetime helping us realize the same.

Gurudev said to His students: I am waiting at the door of Brahmaloka, ready to enter, but I don't want to enter without you all. Hurry up and prepare yourselves. Do your sādhana so that we can all enter together! This is the love of a Jagadguru.

32

Om Jagat-sākṣiṇe Namaḥ

Salutations to the witness of all worldly happenings.

Swami Aparajitananda

Pūjya Gurudev taught us how to remain in the thick of the world, and still be unaffected by the world – padma-patram iva ambhasā – like the lotus leaf in water.

A devotee asked Pūjya Gurudev, "Swamiji! We are saṃsārīs (worldly people). We have possessions and positions, friends and relatives, duties, and responsibilities. How can we saṃsārīs ever progress in spirituality?" Pūjya Gurudev, the Head of several Chinmaya Mission Institutions worldwide, laughed aloud and said: "If worldly activities are to determine a saṃsārī, I should be the greatest saṃsārī!"

How to remain in the world and yet remain unaffected by the world?

Pūjya Gurudev taught us: "Hold on to the Permanent in you and play in the realms of the impermanent; hold on to your real identity – the eternal sākṣī (witnessing Consciousness) in you, and play your role in the drama of the ephemeral jagat (world)!"

A devotee asked, "Swamiji, who is a saṃsārī?" Gurudev replied, "The one who is behind 'some sārī' is a saṃsārī! When we get very much attached to the creation (saṃsāra) and forget the Creator, we become a saṃsārī."

Thanks to the tireless efforts of Pūjya Gurudev for almost four decades, Chinmaya Mission has grown to become a worldwide organization with hundreds of branches and thousands of devotees all over the world.

At the age of seventy-five, even when Gurudev's heart was functioning at only eighteen percent, He was active eighteen hours a day. Even with His failing health, Gurudev's day was fully packed with discourses, meetings, responding to letters, world tours, and so on. An army officer, unable to believe this, once asked Gurudev, "Swamiji, what is the source of your inspiration?" Gurudev, knowing his nature, answered in a language understood by the army officer, "While you take rum, I take Rām!!"

In His later days, an ailing Gurudev who was by then physically old and weak, was approached by an old lady. She expressed her concern, "Swamiji, are you not worried? What will happen to Chinmaya Mission after you are gone?" Gurudev gave a loud laugh and said, "Amma, Chinmaya Mission is His vision, His decision, and His implementation. And if He feels society has benefited from the Mission, He will ensure its future extension and expansion. Why should we go through worry and tension!"

The *Bhagavad-gītā* says that the state of a knower of the Self is that 'I don't do anything'. Om jagat-sākṣiṇe namaḥ – our grateful prostrations to Pūjya Gurudev, who taught us how to abide in the Witness-Bliss within, amidst worldly blisters without.

"When an individual has grown to such a height...and has lost his head in the heights of meditation, he becomes the All-Pervading, because where the ego has ended, the Spirit alone exists. The Spirit needs neither the Eastern spirituality...nor the Western materialism. The Eternal Heart has no continents, no people, and only love. Cultivate such an all-embracing love which seeks no distinction, sees no differences, knows no East and West – and you will bring the whole universe into your palm."
~ Swami Chinmayananda

33

Om Janapriyāya Namaḥ

Salutations to Him, who was loved by all.

Swami Advaitananda

In chapter four of *Kenopaniṣad*, Brahman is described as 'tadvanam', meaning the one that is adorable to all creatures. The Upaniṣad says, the one who meditates on this aspect of Brahman also becomes adorable to all. This is who our Gurudev was. Everyone wanted to seek His blessings, bask in His unconditional love, and be in His uplifting and inspiring company. Since He was abiding in the one eternal Truth, beyond all conditionings, He could love everyone unconditionally. His all-encompassing love, given unconditionally to everyone, made Him the source of joy for everyone. He was loved by all; He was janapriya.

Thousands of devotees all over the world were attracted to Him just like the honeybees gather around a fragrant flower. They felt the urge to bask in Pūjya Gurudev's loving presence. They, not even for a moment, hesitated to serve Gurudev since they identified with Him and considered Him their very own. Here's an incident that showed this aspect clearly:

Gurudev's jñāna yajña was being planned in Mumbai. The organizers realized that the first day of the lecture series fell on the same day as Lakṣmī pūjā. The organizing committee tried to convince Gurudev not to start the yajña on that day because many people might not attend owing to Lakṣmī pūjā in their own homes. However, Gurudev said, "Where Nārāyaṇā is, will Lakṣmī not come?" The yajña started as planned, and around 5,000 people showed up! People loved Him and did not want to miss listening to Him. Many people traveled long distances just to get a glimpse of Him and listen to Him.

Janapriya also means one who loves all. Pūjya Gurudev was not just a realized master but also an ocean of devotion. Gurudev, with a heart that overflowed with love and compassion, offered His sevā to the entire world. No small sevā offered to Him went unnoticed. Wherever Gurudev traveled, He recognized the contribution of everyone who took care of Him, from the host to the driver, the gardener, or the cook. He showered His love unconditionally upon all. *Tulasī Rāmāyaṇa* describes a devotee as "sab ke priya sab ke hitkārī" – a devotee is one who is loved by all and who is ever engaged in the welfare of all beings. Sage Vālmīki says in the *Rāmāyaṇa* that God dwells in the hearts of such great devotees. *Rāmāyaṇa* is thus describing our Gurudev, who worked tirelessly throughout His life for the well-being of people. Even with fragile health, He continued to work, meet with people, give talks, and was easily accessible to everyone.

No wonder He was janapriya. Our humble salutations to Him, who loved all and was loved by all.

"Whenever a free minute or two appeared in his demanding schedule, he would slip away to sit at his desk, picking up, without a moment's hesitation, exactly where he had left off his work before. Whether on the lecture platform or at his desk or in a meeting in his āśrama office, his approach to work was always the same: He reveled in the very doing of it. From the glow on his face and the joy in his limbs, you could see that his work was, indeed, love made visible."

~ Rudite Emir

34

Om Jitendriyāya Namaḥ

Salutations to the one who conquered all the sense organs.

Swami Anukoolananda

Each name of Pūjya Gurudev's Aṣṭottara Śata Nāmāvali carries a profound message. At once, it describes Gurudev's transcendental nature, and in the same breath, it points out to us, His devotees, an important sādhana.

Amidst all comforts, abundance, and even luxury, are we truly free? Until we have conquered ourselves, the world will continue to dictate our life's tribulations.

A seeker should learn to live with things and without things. A sincere seeker should be alert, lest he gets used to having few things. The mind will start demanding them, and ere long make him helplessly dependent on them. Dependency is the root of all misery.

A true master will be equanimous with everything around and with nothing around. "Win the mind, win the world", roared Pūjya Gurudev in His countless *Bhagavad-gītā* lectures across the world. Pūjya Gurudev was truly a 'jitendriya' – a conqueror and a master of His 'indriyas' – the senses outside and the mind within.

The luxuries of childhood did not daunt Balan's readiness to endure the endless tortures of the freedom struggle, nor did His body and mind protest the severe deprivation during His spiritual quest. The comforts and grandeur that played around later, appeared only as mere fancies around Gurudev, the epitome of detachment.

Gurudev lived uncompromisingly, waking up at the brahma muhurta every morning. His loud chanting of 'Om' echoed in every palatial house that He stayed in. The practice of the pre-dawn meditation was non-negotiable, even at His advanced age and precarious health.

The tough life of the Himalayas prepared Gurudev well for His endless struggles in the early days of His missionary work. With no assurance of the next meal, nor people or resources for the next program, Gurudev rallied on relentlessly, fearless, and unperturbed. Once we have handled deprivation well, abundance will no longer wield any magic to tantalize us.

Detachment and non-dependency were Gurudev's most powerful weapons and were evident in every aspect of Gurudev's life. Gurudev was once asked, "Your organization is expanding rapidly. What will happen to it when you are gone?" Pat came Gurudev's reply, "I don't care what will happen to it, even when I am there!" Gurudev considered even this organization as only another tool in His vast vision and work that He undertook in His lifetime for the Hindu renaissance.

We have heard another anecdote of Gurudev, where He continued the discourse in spite of His bleeding foot, torn by a nail that it had struck while ascending to the Vyāsa pīṭha. The precarious health condition of the later years could not dampen even a bit of Gurudev's joyous spirit nor His boundless eagerness to serve the cause of Hindu revival.

May this great mastery of the senses and the mind that Pūjya Gurudev demonstrated His entire life uplift the intensity of our efforts at Hindu revival and, ultimately, our struggle for liberation.

35

Om Jīvabrahmaikyavide Namaḥ

Salutations to the knower of oneness of the individual and the Supreme.

Swami Aparokshananda

In Vedānta, there is an illustration of a room with four walls, a ceiling, and a floor. When we look at it, we label the room as large, small, clean, or dirty. All these labels are given because we focus our attention on the walls and floor. If we were to shift our attention to the actual space, we would recognize that it is neither clean nor dirty and, in fact, not large or small. The very space inside the room is the same space that is outside the room and stretches into the infinite universe.

In the same way, the jīva is consciousness that appears to be confined within the walls of the body-mind-intellect (BMI). When we focus on the BMI, we see ourselves as tall, short, happy, sad, smart, or dull. However, when we shift our attention to the consciousness within, we realize that it has none of these attributes and is, in fact, infinite. This infinite Consciousness is called 'Brahman'. A person who knows that this jīva consciousness is, in fact, one with the infinite consciousness 'Brahman' is a jīvabrahmaikyavid. This is not theoretical knowledge but a deep doubt-free conviction that 'I am that infinite Consciousness' (ahaṁ brahmāsmi).

When a person achieves this level of spiritual perfection, then he or she lives beyond all labels of short, tall, happy, sad, smart, or dull. They no longer label or believe themselves to be limited and live a life of courage and freedom. Such was our master, Swami Chinmayananda, who abided in this knowledge at all times. He was courageous enough to leave the divine quietude of the Himalayas to spread this precious knowledge to all. He was courageous enough to overcome all the obstacles ahead of a grand plan of spiritual upliftment for mankind. But most importantly, He was courageous enough to wholeheartedly love all those who had the great fortune to meet Him.

Most of us live inside the 'small room' feeling unloved and scared to love others. We then try to impress, compare, and complain about others and how they don't love us enough. If only we could see ourselves as endless consciousness, peace, and bliss that pervades the BMI and spreads to the limitless regions of time and space, we wouldn't feel scared to love others or desperately pant for them to love us.

Gurudev was one such master who conquered all with His love. Never waiting to be loved, His creed was 'happiness depends on what you can give, not on what you get'. Give, give, give – He did. Love, love, love – He did and still does. If we can close our eyes and look within, we can meet Him there and feel the courage to embrace the world with love and kindness.

"Shattering the barriers between the Macrocosm and the Microcosm to authoritatively declare that they are one and the same; imploring Seekers to go beyond the mere rote learning of scriptural grammar to transform every teaching into an irrefutable direct experience of Self, by roaring at every opportune moment He gets –
'Tat Tvam Asi' - Realize that!"
~ Source: Chinmaya Ashtottara Namavali,
Chinmaya YouTube Channel

36

Om Jīvanmuktāya Namaḥ

Salutations to the one who is liberated.

Swami Devatmananda

As I sit at Tapovan Kutir in Uttarkashi, I cannot but marvel and bow my head with utmost reverence to Pūjya Tapovan Maharaj and Pūjya Gurudev Swami Chinmayananda for all the qualities they embodied, their mastery in Vedānta and their abidance in the Self. They are proof to society that one can be liberated while living in this body. Their lives inspire millions of seekers to aspire to be liberated while living in this perishable body.

- om – The Absolute Truth
- śrī – blessed with the wealth of knowledge, wealth of guṇas, and wealth of the world.
- jīvan – living in the perishable body
- muktāya – absolutely free from all bondages.
  He lives in the perishable body, uplifting humankind with the knowledge of His real svarūpa, Sat-Cit-Ānanda, Om.

Bondage is caused by the ignorance of our true nature and by the erroneous identification with the BMI (Body, Mind, and Intellect). A liberated person or a jīvanmukta has woken up to His true Nature, realizing that there is only one Reality (Brahman) with the many seeming reflections of the One Reality (jīvas), just like the dreamer wakes up from sleep to realize the oneness between the dreamer and waker. With the knowledge of His true Identity, He moves in the world with infinite compassion, love, and kindness uplifting everyone along the way. Śrī Kṛṣṇa declares to Arjuna:

yogasannyastakarmāṇaṁ jñānasañchinnasaṁśayam,
ātmavantaṁ na karmāṇi nibadhnanti dhanañjaya.

"Actions do not bind those who have renounced actions in yoga, whose doubts have been dispelled by knowledge, and who are abiding in the knowledge of the Self." (Bhagavad-gītā 4.41)

This was very evident in Pūjya Gurudev, who was ever established in the knowledge of Self as He worked dynamically for more than eighteen hours a day without being bound by any of those actions. He worked tirelessly, providing all the tools necessary for people of all ages to evolve spiritually and to experience the Reality that He had experienced by the grace of His Gurus, Swami Tapovan Maharaj and Swami Sivananda Maharaj.

Let us invoke Pūjya Gurudev's grace to walk the path shown by Him to one day reach our goal of being free from all bondages.

> *"The Man of Perfection is like a breeze that passes by without asking. When the windows are open, it purifies the atmosphere by its mere passing. It changes its direction when the windows are closed."*
> *~ Swami Chinmayananda*

na tatra cakṣurgacchati na vāggacchati no manaḥ,
na vidmo na vijānīmo yathaitadanuśiṣyāt,
anyadeva tadviditādatho aviditādadhi,
iti śuśruma pūrveṣāṃ ye nastadvyācacakṣire.

The eye does not go there, nor speech, nor mind. We do not know That. We do not know how to instruct one about It. It is distinct from the known and above the unknown. We have heard it, so stated the preceptors who taught us That.

~ *Kenopaniṣad* 3

37

Om Jīrṇa-mandira-uddhārakāya Namaḥ

Salutations to the renovator of dilapidated temples and rejuvenator of Hindu culture.

Swami Gunatitananda

Jīrṇa-mandira-uddhāraka means one who uplifted or revived temples. It was no secret that Pūjya Gurudev was involved not only in the revival of many dilapidated Hindu temples but also in building new temples. His contribution towards the revival of the temples was not merely limited to the brick and mortar used to construct the temple or the work and the funds associated with it.

Traditionally, temples were the source of spirituality through knowledge and practice. However, due to colonialism, ignorance, and decadence, the significance of the temples was gradually lost along with their physical deterioration. Pūjya Gurudev played a crucial role by not only renovating the temples and building new temples but also by reviving their significance in the minds of Hindus by making them aware of their heritage through Bala Vihar, Chinmaya Yuva Kendra, study classes for adults, and spiritual discourses. He used to say that religion is a combination of philosophy and rituals (theory and practice), and one can't be without the other. Most Hindu rituals were becoming (or in danger of becoming) superstitions due to a lack of knowledge of the philosophy behind them, which was one of the reasons for the deterioration of the Hindu temples. Hindu traditions and temples were becoming easy targets of ridicule by other faiths. Re-educating Hindus about the philosophy behind the rituals was part of His mission, which was essential to ensure that the Hindu temples withstood the onslaught of not mere natural degeneration but the forces that tried to undermine Hinduism.

Pūjya Gurudev's role in the revival of the temples did not stop with the aspects that focused on mere physical structures. A temple is where God resides. Upaniṣads declare, "You Are That," and you can meet your Self or God in your own heart – implying that though God is everywhere, you can know God or Self only in your heart – one's heart is God's ultimate temple. This knowledge was almost lost over a period of time for many reasons. Pūjya Gurudev led the spiritual renaissance of the individuals by taking this highest knowledge contained in the Upaniṣads to the doorsteps of Hindus, wherever they lived, through His jñāna-yajñas (spiritual discourses), thereby playing a vital role in elevating their minds from misinterpretations of our śāstras and re-establishing the temple in their hearts, paving the way for Self-realization or God-realization.

At the physical level, Pūjya Gurudev revived the temples with brick-and-mortar funds and hard work. He also ensured that the revival efforts were long-lasting by reviving Sanātana Dharma (Hinduism) and its traditions. Further, He also ensured the revival of the ultimate temple of God in the hearts of the individuals by rekindling the fire of knowledge of the Self, as stated in the Upaniṣads. It is no wonder Pūjya Gurudev is aptly called jīrṇa-mandira-uddhāraka because He was, is, and will be in every way a torch-bearer in the revival efforts of our temples.

38

Om Tapovanaśiṣyāya Namaḥ

Salutations to the disciple of Swami Tapovan Maharaj.

Dev Singh

Swami Tapovan Maharaj was Pūjya Gurudev Swami Chinmayananda's śikṣā guru. It was from Him that Pūjya Gurudev learned the scriptures, and later revived them to inspire and transform so many people all over the world.

From texts like *Ishwara Darshan* and *Wandering in The Himalayas*, one gets a glimpse into why Swami Tapovan Maharaj was regarded as Himavat Vibhūti (the glory of the Himalayas). We are fortunate to have all received the sacred and rare gift of His blessings, grace, guidance, and support in our daily sādhana, brought to us from the Himalayas in the form of Pūjya Gurudev. Remembering this blessing alone promises enough inspiration and courage to live rightly and follow this path to grow out of our selfishness and delusions.

Swami Tapovan Maharaj, a stalwart in Vedānta, was recognized by many saints as the personification of the Reality and the one with all the virtues described in our scriptures. He was respected among saints, kings, and foreigners. It is described that all the sannyāsīs that the Himalayas could muster, gathered together like an ocean of orange in a show of reverence at His jal mahāsamādhi. The king and the queen of Nepal regularly sought His guidance, and the British, who respected His vast knowledge of the Purāṇas and Himalayan topography, named the Tapovanam mountain after Him in recognition of His majestic greatness.

One of the meanings of the word 'tapovan' indicates the one who is a forest of austerities; His life was one of indescribable and divine tapas from every point of view.

Pūjya Gurudev's words about Swami Tapovan Maharaj are both instructive and inspiring. Once, a devotee asked Gurudev, "Tell us something about Swami Tapovan Maharaj." Gurudev kept quiet for a long time and said, "In whom, I became silent." Can there be better words to describe one's Guru? Reflecting on this, we are compelled to acknowledge that to remain in the joyous glory that is our most beloved Guru, we must continue to strive to meet Him there in that same silence.

At another time, Gurudev shared, "All my life is a story of my love for Him." It is interesting that Pūjya Gurudev appears so different from Swami Tapovanam. While Swami Tapovan Maharaj remained a recluse in the Himalayas, Pūjya Gurudev traversed the whole world, teaching all ages in all ways envisioning and implementing novel institutions and programs for generations to come. However, one can see the grace of Bhagavān in the form of the Guru-tattva in both of Them, flowing down to reach all. Both the Master and His disciple were perfect Gurus as described in the scriptures, full of compassion, teaching the Truth with every breath, with one voice, in different ways to different jīvas everywhere.

Only a few people have ever directly met or heard Swami Tapovanam. Yet, His wisdom, purity, and austerity have gotten into our sādhana and our personalities. It speaks to how our Pūjya Gurudev, a perfect śiṣya, has brought Swami Tapovanam, the epitome of Guru parampara, into our lives.

39

Om Tapasvine Namaḥ

Salutations to the austere ascetic.

Swami Prakashananda

Tapa in Sanskrit means to burn. A tapasvi, as our Pūjya Gurudev is described here, is one who has subjected Himself to the rigors and hardships of austerities and sādhana and has burnt away all sancita (accumulated) karmas – a jīvanmukta.

Tapas is characterized by sternness and severity in spiritual pursuit. Hence, the burning. When the mind and body do not want to do something because it is uncomfortable, at that time to subject them to discipline, hardship, sternness, severity, and rigor is called tapas for a seeker. The result is evolution. It requires sacrificing the lower for the higher by subjecting the BMI (Body-Mind-Intellect) to discipline and rigor.

All metamorphosis burns (involves pain or difficulty). In the *Taittirīya-upaniṣad*, it is said that the Reality Itself underwent tapas and manifested this jagat (universe). The imperishable blissful Reality – Paramātmā – subjects Itself to Its own power of māyā and appears finite and perishable, subjected to sorrows as though.

Pūjya Gurudev, by His accounts (*My Trek Through Uttarakhand*), subjected His BMI to various rigorous tapas, removing the last remnants of saṃsārik fetters. Just like cream of milk or coconut milk, when subjected to the heat of fire, results in a pure, clean product – ghee and coconut oil respectively; Pūjya Gurudev became for us the example of one who is the pure product of the heating process of tapas. The Reality underwent tapas and manifested as this Universe. Gurudev underwent tapas and is still manifesting Chinmaya Mission across the globe. All tapas results in great things!

In the *Kaṭhopaniṣad* (1.3.1), the Reality Itself is called tapa by the ṛṣis! In this context, the word tapa means the light of consciousness, responsible for citchāyā (reflected consciousness), the jīva. Sat is existence. It doesn't give the sense of life or knowledge. Cit, however, conveys a more dynamic sense of the Reality because it enlivens and brings vivacity, dynamism, heartiness, and vigor! These words are the most apt descriptions of our Gurudev.

From this standpoint, our Pūjya Gurudev is the 'Cit' aspect of Paramātmā Himself! No wonder the Reality chose to go by the name Chinmaya! But He taught us that we are all Paramātmā! The difference is for Gurudev, it was His realization, and for us, it is merely knowledge gathered through śravaṇam.

Like our Gurudev did, the śāstras thunder, "Thou art That!" It has only been ingested. It has to be digested, absorbed, assimilated, metabolized, and manifested as bliss Absolute. He walked the path and did it. For forty years, He did tapas to show us the path. In the shadow of the grace of Paramātmā, manifested as our Gurudev, we continue our tapas, walking the path and hoping to lift the veil of ignorance and realize So'ham – I am He!

Salutations to that great Tapasvi!

40

Om Tāpanāśanāya Namaḥ

Salutations to the destroyer of sorrows.

Swami Ramakrishnananda

Pūjya Gurudev Swami Chinmayananda, burning with a passion to serve the people, came to Pune from the Himalayas in 1951. At a time when service was associated with social activities alone, He shared the knowledge of the Self. So why did Pūjya Gurudev embark on this different mission to serve people?

Running away from worries and towards happiness is the goal of every soul in this universe. Our scriptures classify the problems and worries of life into these three categories: (1) ādhyātmika tāpa – worries due to bodily suffering and mental anguish; (2) ādibhautika tāpa – worries caused by other beings; (3) ādidaivika tāpa – worries due to unseen divine forces that we have no control over. Man is always striving to get out of worries in pursuit of happiness. He looks for solutions that are most often easy and pleasant but soon realizes that the perceived solutions actually lead to more problems. When he finds the right means or path to get away from his worries, he attains eternal happiness. Worries emerge from a wrong understanding of ourselves and wrong judgment about things and beings around us, the root cause of which is ignorance. Once ignorance is eliminated, wrong understanding and judgment, and worries will be rooted out completely and permanently.

Śrī Ādi Śankarācārya, says in the *Bhagavad-gītā*, "Worry is the product of delusion; moha brings śoka." Śrī

Kṛṣṇa eliminated the delusion of Arjuna by giving him the knowledge of the Self. Pūjya Gurudev analyzed the life of human beings in the modern world and understood the various problems of man. He knew that only Self-knowledge could give permanent solutions for all mental worries, and also bring the best out of every individual which in turn contributes to a healthy and happy nation.

Swami Chinmayananda traveled all over the world to spread the wisdom and knowledge of our scriptures, dispelling the delusion and ignorance from the hearts of human beings. Upaniṣads and the *Bhagavad-gītā* became His powerful weapons to destroy the worries of mankind. In this journey, He brought together hundreds of well-trained workers, to do His work; Gurudev's work continues and reminds us of the Motto that He envisioned – 'Maximum happiness for the maximum people for the maximum time'.

Gurudev worked tirelessly for the welfare of human beings by authoring books, building spiritual centers and schools, and conducting jñāna-yajñas. He educated people of all ages through Bala Vihar, study groups, and so on, and created an army of Brahmacārins who can continue His vision to spread the ancient knowledge to every nook of the world. All the spiritual and cultural work done in His lifetime was only to eliminate the worries and pains of humanity.

Ādi Śankarācārya says in *Vivekacūḍāmaṇi,* 'vasantavat lokahitam caranti' – saintly people move in this world like spring season to give happiness to all. Pūjya Gurudev Swami Chinmayananda also moved in this world like the 'vasanta ṛtu' removing pains and giving happiness to all.

41

Om Tīrthasvarūpāya Namaḥ

Salutations to the one who is a scared place of pilgrimage in Himself.

Brahmacharini Vrindha Chaitanya

The Lord is all-pervading, but where His presence, expression, omnipotence, grace, and blessing capacity vividly manifests is called tīrtha. Hence, a tīrtha is laden with the power to sanctify everyone.

Our scriptures glorify the Guru as the ādhibhautika, ādhidaivika, and ādhyātmika tīrtha and state that a Guru is intrinsically the absolute Self. Pūjya Gurudev was such a spiritual Master.

Once, a devotee expressed her grief to Pūjya Gurudev for not being able to go on a pilgrimage she had earnestly desired and planned for. In response, Pūjya Gurudev said that coming to one's Guru is equivalent to all pilgrimages, reiterating what Lord Śiva says in *Guru-gītā* – sarvatīrthamayaṃ devi śrīguroścaraṇāmbujam. Further, *Śrīmad Bhāgavatam,* as well as *Nārada Bhakti Sūtra* say – tīrthīkurvanti tīrthāni – a tīrtha also owes its sanctity and existence to saints, as they alone manifest the Lord with their love and austerity. Because of Pūjya Gurudev alone, Lord Hanuman graced Sidhbari with His magnificent form, and it became a recognized tīrtha. Mother Ganga agreed to descend upon earth due to the assurance of the touch of saints, who would sustain Her purity, even after innumerable sinners bathe in Her. The very physical presence of Gurudev brought peace and solace to many. His discipline as a teacher helped seekers overcome negligence, and His loving embrace freed them from fears and self-doubt.

In *Śrī Rāmacaritamānasa*, Gosvāmī Tulasīdāsa says that the Guru is the Lord Himself, the ocean of compassion who has assumed human form. *Guru-gītā* also says that the Guru and Lord Śiva are one. Differentiating between the two and limiting the Guru to the mortal form is a grave sin. Thus, Pūjya Gurudev is Lord Śiva incarnate, and His lordliness is intrinsic to the very address 'Gurudev'.

As the whole cosmos is the manifestation of the Lord's saṅkalpa, the entire Chinmaya Mission, encompassing hundreds of centers across the globe, educational institutions, hospitals, and various other initiatives and projects, is the manifestation of the saṅkalpa śakti of one Master alone.

The Guru knows the mind and the intellect of a disciple threadbare. Upon surrender, He imparts guidance, the means to evolution, and ultimately, the knowledge of the Self to free the disciple from ignorance and identification with the wrong 'I'. By pervading the disciple's mind and intellect, the Guru alone purifies and liberates the disciple.

Pūjya Gurudev was called the walking-talking *Gītā*. Be it the qualities of a devotee or the characteristics of a Man of realization, He personified it all and lived all the teachings of the *Bhagavad-gītā*.

Pūjya Gurudev is intrinsically a tīrtha svarūpa. He descended to the plains and traveled far and wide like Mother Ganga to fearlessly take the knowledge of the scriptures to the masses as He was established in the ever-pure, untainted sacred Self.

42

Om Tejasvine Namaḥ

Salutations to the brilliant one.

Brahmachari Anand Chaitanya

"I am the midday sun. You can see its light, but you cannot see it. You can only see the rising and setting sun." These are Pūjya Gurudev Swami Chinmayananda's words. One can see anything only with the light of the Self, but one cannot see the Self itself. Swamiji's words are from His own experience of the source of all lights.

Gurudev always operated from awareness and alertness and gave His best even in a seemingly insignificant action. Gurudev expected us to 'Do the best and leave the rest'. The word tejas alludes to light or brilliance, which is the nature of sattva guṇa. One in whom sattva guṇa is dominant will always be selfless and work dynamically towards a noble cause. Gurudev created a vast sāttvik infrastructure in the form of an organization so that others could study, serve, and eventually achieve what He had achieved.

As advised by His Guru, Shri Tapovan Maharaj, Gurudev kept His teachings simple and direct so that the common man could connect and practice the subtle and more profound lessons embodied in our scriptures. He designed the simple and widely known BMI chart (Body-Mind-Intellect) to explain the profundity of our scriptures. The divine Om to anything in the realm of matter can be indicated through the BMI chart. Consistent study and practice of scriptures makes us more sāttvik giving us clarity in thinking and courage in action.

Gurudev inspired tens of thousands of people through His scriptural teachings. He set many standards for others to follow and reach that Divinity, which is one's true Nature. His messages had a special impact on the youth. He said, "Keep your goal so high that you can never reach the goal." The process of striving towards the goal can help one attain transformation in life. On another occasion, He said, "Bring your mind to where your hands are." These words of Swamiji can lend both beauty and meaning to even small acts that we undertake. When we have a higher vision and the right attitude to execute it, life becomes brilliant. Gurudev echoed the famous message of ṛṣis, 'tejasvi nāvadhītamastu', when He said, "Efficiency is the capacity to bring proficiency into action."

In the decades following independence, He ventured into the noble task of uplifting people spiritually and culturally when it was most needed in Bhārat. To steer the thinking of the educated Indians towards 'Bhārat' and Hindu-ness was the need of the hour. Gurudev's brilliance can be seen in the avenues of spirituality. He created Bala Vihar, Chinmaya Yuva Kendra, Chinmaya Devi Group, and Chinmaya Vanaprastha – all meant for family members of different age groups. After all, the family is the unit of the Bhāratīya society, not the individual.

Our ṛṣis had the great vision of universal Oneness. For this universal vision of 'World is One Family' to exist and be made available to all, our ancient Sanātana Dharma or Hinduism must be revived and preserved. This is the most brilliant and sāttvik ideology to sustain peace in the world. As a true yogī and ṛṣi, Swamiji consistently made the effort to revive Hinduism and awaken the masses to realize the true spirit and potential of Sanātana Dharma.

43

Om Dehātītāya Namaḥ

Salutations to the one who is beyond the body.

Swami Siddhananda

A man of realization has a clear conviction that He is not the body, mind, and intellect. Instead, He uses the body, mind, and intellect diligently, intelligently, and efficiently as instruments to serve humanity. In Gurudev's words, "When I say that I am not the body, I am NOT the body!"

Gurudev never used to celebrate His birthday. His ṣaṣṭiabdapūrti (sixtieth birthday) was arranged by devotees in a very simple way in Coimbatore. His pūjā and japa were *Gītā* jñāna-yajñas. His likhita japa was writing letters to His devotees. His favorite text was Śrī Ādi Śankarācārya's *Vivekacūḍāmaṇi*, and His favorite ślokas were the famous meditation verses from *Vivekacūḍāmaṇi* – "jāti nīti kula gotra dūragam" (Brahman is beyond caste, names and forms, good and bad, space and time). His favorite stotram was Tapovana Ṣatkam.

Once, Gurudev came to Chinmaya Mission Tri-State Center, Kedar, in Philadelphia, after His eye surgery. The inauguration of the Chinmaya Kedar Center was happening the next day. Gurudev attended the inauguration and did not hesitate to remove His eye bandage to see the big oil lamps lit in front of Lord Kedāreśvara.

On another occasion, Gurudev was in Delhi for a yajña. On the second day, He fell ill with a high fever and cold, and was unable to get up due to high body temperature. The committee approached Him and asked if they should cancel the yajña. Despite the pain, Gurudev said the program should go as planned. He finally agreed to cancel just that day but insisted that the session continue with a disciple. He was dehātīta and worked tirelessly without paying heed to physical illness. The ocher-colored clothes He wore symbolized how the body comes from clay and goes back to clay.

True knowledge enables a man to realize that he is the soul with a body. He is unborn, so, he never dies. The way Gurudev walked in His pādukās, His rudrākṣa mālās, the vibhūti and chandan on His forehead, His loud laughter, unconditional love, and sevā, continue to live in our minds and hearts.

Gurudev is still looking after all of us; the centers are growing, and the community is thriving with His blessings. He is 'dehātīta'; His physical body may not be here, but the legacy He left behind continues to guide us in various ways.

"Made up of the five elements, the body is a nest of diseases and pains. To cater to its demands can be a twelve-month, twenty-four-hour job, and yet it will suffer. Use it as an instrument for sevā of others. Trees give fruit to others; the tree eats none. The river never drinks but its waters are meant for plants, animals, and humans. The sun, the wind – look around. In nature, man alone wants to live for himself and perpetuate! Leave it alone. Let the body run its course. Let us live our life peacefully in Him, the Bliss. Look after the body as a workman tends to his instruments."

~ Swami Chinmayananda

44

Om Dvandvātītāya Namaḥ

Salutations to the one who is beyond the pairs of opposites.

Swamini Aaradhanananda

On the battlefield, Arjuna asks Śrī Kṛṣṇa to describe the state of a sthitaprajña. Superficially, it may seem that he is asking about an enlightened soul's demeanor of how he sits, talks, walks, and so on. But on a deeper level, he is eager to know about the sādhana of such a person as stated in the Vedānta – śravaṇam (listening to the scriptural teachings) that clears his prajña of ignorance; mananam (reflection) that makes him a man of steady and mature intellect; and samādhī (meditation) that leads him to the ultimate experience.

Śrī Kṛṣṇa asserts that one of the prime qualities of a sthitaprajña is that he is beyond the vicissitudes of dualities that can toss and tamper our peace of mind. He is unperturbed by dvandvas, the dualities that play out in our life. Sorrow and joy can't make him dance to their tunes.

We experience dualities at three levels:

(1) at the physical level: heat and cold, health and illness.

(2) at the emotional level: sadness and happiness.

(3) at the intellectual level: honor and dishonor.

How did our matchless Master, our own beloved Swami Chinmayananda sail through the onslaught of dualities on His body, mind, and intellect?

At the physical level: Despite His heart functioning only at twenty percent, Pūjya Gurudev's magnificent roaring of the scriptural truths from the podium is legendary. He was once waiting on a stinky railway station platform for the arrival of a delayed train. He refused people fanning Him to ward off flies. When a disciple asked why He wasn't covering His nostrils, to avoid inhaling the stench, He answered, "Your attention is on the foul-smelling air, and mine is on the element of space. It is detached, so no odor emanates from it."

At the emotional level: Mother Ganga whispered in Gurudev's ears, that, like Her, He should go down to the plains to spread the knowledge of Vedānta far and wide. Initially, this "English-speaking monk" wasn't welcomed by traditionalists, who weren't aware of His prowess or intentions. But Pūjya Gurudev was way above insults and insinuations.

At the intellectual level: A radical reformer that Pūjya Gurudev was, many raised their eyebrows, when He opened Sandeepany Sadhanalaya to women too. He stuck to His decision, braving criticism.

If only we could imbibe a modicum of His wisdom, a semblance of His balance, our thoughts, words, and deeds would emit the fragrance of love and harmony in this world.

"Equipoise is a state of mental equilibrium that comes when one has unshakeable intellectual foundations and the mental capacity to soar to the highest pinnacles of greater visions. When a person raises himself into greater ambits of spiritual vision, his mind will no longer entertain any agitations at the ordinary level of likes and dislikes. None of the happenings at the level of the mind and intellect can be of any serious consequence to a person who is trying to detach from the dualistic experiences and who has learned the art of drawing inspiration from something beyond."

~ Swami Chinmayananda

45

Om Dṛḍhaniścayāya Namaḥ

Salutations to Him, who is of firm resolve.

Swamini Sampratishtananda

Dṛḍha means firm, and niścaya means resolve, determination, and conviction. It is this value that keeps our mind steady on the goal and inspires us to keep moving forward despite any obstacles that may come. To a jñāni puruṣa, this is a virtue and is natural, as seen in Pūjya Gurudev at all levels.

At the transactional level, for any achievement, firm conviction is required. We find this quality manifesting in Gurudev even as a student in college, as a freedom fighter, and as a journalist.

As a seeker, a firm conviction that there is a Reality and that I can realize it through the valid means of knowledge – Vedānta as expounded by my Guru – is absolutely essential.

At the highest level, there should be a firm conviction that the nature of Reality is Existence-Consciousness-Bliss, and that is Me, the supreme Self. What is the need for firm conviction? Only when I know the value or preciousness of something do I desire it and resolve to get it, whether the way is conducive or otherwise. The stronger the conviction, the greater my efforts to achieve it.

Gurudev pursued this knowledge till it culminated in the Realization of the Self. On being guided to Swami Tapovan Maharaj for a deeper study of the scriptures, Gurudev walked from Rishikesh to Uttarkashi through forests and wild paths. He reached Uttarkashi after many days only to be told by

Tapovan Maharaj to get an introductory letter from Swami Sivananda. Undeterred, Gurudev went back to Rishikesh and got the letter. Swami Tapovan Maharaj was in no hurry to start teaching the eager student, putting it off for a month. Later, he wanted Gurudev to make a vegetable garden near the kuṭiyā. Water was available only after a steep climb of around 100 feet and had to be fetched in buckets from the river. This is similar to the *Praśnopaniṣad* student who was aṣked to wait and serve. The student, with firm resolve, performs all the chores that are expected of him. The student may not understand the why and the what in the Guru's words. But his resolve is so firm that nothing will deter him from the path chosen, and his faith in his Guru only gets strengthened by the day. Gurudev stopped short of nothing to plunge within and move beyond cravings of body-mind-intellect to the very source of truth within, where Peace, Existence, Consciousness, and Bliss are seen as the Self.

This yuga puruṣa resolved to share this knowledge with the masses, taking inspiration from Mother Ganga with the blessings of His Guru. He came down to the plains with no money, no materials, and no men to help. He remained firm and focused in teaching the message of the *Bhagavad-gītā* and Upaniṣads, with a heart filled with love and compassion, from the year 1951 till His body gave up in 1993.

May Gurudev bless us abundantly to walk the path He took – a path of dedicated service, the study of scriptures, following the instructions given therein, and having a firm resolve for this great knowledge.

46

Om Dharmasaṁsthāpakāya Namaḥ

Salutations to the one who establishes dharma.

Swamini Supriyananda

Dharma may be understood at various levels. For starters, dharma represents the moral values that religions prescribe; in essence, that which is right or good. It also represents our duty. To elaborate, individuals have continually and constantly been receiving from the moment of their conception. As such, a duty is owed to give back for all that has been received and to all those who have provided. Whilst one recognizes that certain things cannot be paid back in the same measure or way, dharma promotes giving back innate, immeasurable values, such as time, skills, and love.

Dharma can be seen as the eternal laws that govern all of creation, like the laws discovered by science, and also the laws the scriptures proffer as guidance on how to live our lives. Additionally, dharma is the glue that holds things together – the unifying force. In the same way that virtues hold a family in place, dharma keeps meaning, purpose, and truth positionally intact. Lastly, dharma is the essential nature of an object. For example, the dharma of sugar is sweetness.

Pūjya Gurudev re-established dharma at all these aforementioned varying interpretations, being true to the name 'dharma samsthāpaka'. To start with, Bala Vihar was a place that introduced not only values and human goodness but also the quality of viveka – the ability to discriminate right from wrong. Gurudev prompted this understanding by using lively stories to make the knowledge easily available. He not only wrote commentaries on scriptures, which ultimately materialized in numerous notable books but also answered hundreds of letters every day to tailor a more personal and situational-specific response.

Gurudev deftly expanded on dharma as a duty. With the oft-association of duty with obligation, one instantly assumes duty to be a tiring and unpleasant task that is forced upon an individual. However, one begins to gain awareness of what has been received and, stemming from gratitude, of wanting to give back. In His light-hearted way of teaching, using English as the main mode of communication, He beautifully re-established dharma as the eternal law by bringing the scriptures alive. His teachings were easily understood, accepted, and respected. To facilitate the process of giving back, Gurudev set up opportunities to help by serving in the mission or by engaging in projects that pertained to schools, hospitals, and rural development. He further built āśramas and temples to allow us to give back to the ṛṣi culture as an acknowledgment of all the wisdom that we have received.

Finally, He presented an understanding of dharma by reflecting on both sva-dharma and what is our essential dharma as divine beings. Acting in accordance with one's sva-dharma, an individual truly blossoms and feels fulfilled in their actions. Beyond this, our essential dharma is to delve into a deeper level, where everyone exists as spiritual beings who have human experiences but recognize that their nature is divinity. The goal of life is to discover this essential nature and live in that joy, love, and peace, and the first step to attaining this state, as inspired by Gurudev, is knowledge.

47

Om Dhīmate Namaḥ

Salutations to the intelligent and discriminate one.

Swamini Amritananda

Dhīmate – the one who is dhīmān, the intelligent one. Dhīmān is one who has an acute sense of discernment (viveka), as it is this faculty of the intellect, conferred to us as humans alone, that sets us apart from the animal kingdom.

Pūjya Gurudev would often describe humans as belonging to one of three categories: animal-man, man-man, and God-man. Dhīmān is one who has recognized the true potential of human birth and has made oneself a God-man or is on the path of spiritual evolution from a man-man to a God-man using their viveka. Life presents us with two choices at every moment – the path of pleasure (preyas) and the path of good (śreyas). An intelligent individual chooses the path of the good at every turn, while the dull chooses the path of pleasure as a result of their short-term thinking, acquiring and protecting material objects in hopes of happiness. However, the intelligent individual makes choices not based on what is easy and pleasurable but that which is good, that which brings fulfillment and happiness to oneself and others in the long run. The *Kaṭhopaniṣad* calls such an individual a dhīraḥ, and Śrī Ādi Śankarācārya calls him a dhīmān.

Having realized the shortcomings of western education appreciated by society, discontent with a successful career, and frustrated with the hollowness of lavish living with world name and fame, Balakrishna Menon yearned for a more fulfilling life, not only for himself but also to share his insights for the benefit of all – being the journalist that he was! Stumbling by accident upon Swami Sivananda of the Divine Life Society and his works, Balakrishna Menon found answers that he had been seeking all his life. Recognizing the life lived by the sādhus as a much better scheme of living, he at once took to changing his lifestyle and brought it in accordance with the teachings of the Master and the scriptures. Not content with mere external achievement, he sought to realize the Truth himself and was willing to do all that was required, even if it meant walking away from all he had worked for his entire life and taking sannyāsa.

In the *Bhagavad-gītā* (2.15), the Lord describes the man who is equanimous in joy and sorrow as the most fit to gain immortality. Śrī Ādi Śankarācārya calls such a person a dhīmān or one with a well-endowed intellect. Understanding the goal of life to be much greater than the passing temporary experiences, the dhīmān, do not get deterred from the goal, nor do they get caught up in the oscillations of the mind, even temporarily. Pūjya Gurudev's life was exemplary of this quality. Whether it was fighting for Bhārat's freedom from the British and having to live on the run, spending time in prison for his activism, or studying the scriptures in the harsh conditions of Uttarkashi with little to no comforts, once a goal was set, no external situations would deter Gurudev from achieving it. Invoking that same quality, Pūjya Gurudev brought to us our greatest blessing – the deep meaning of the scriptures in a language and style appealing to us despite staunch opposition and criticism from fellow sādhus.

Pūjya Gurudev lived a life that became, for us, a blueprint of intelligent living. Our salutations to the intelligent one; may His blessings guide us to live intelligently, and also come to rediscover our own divinity.

48

Om Dhīrāya Namaḥ

Salutations to the courageous one who walks the righteous path.

Brahmacharini Robyn Thompson

We prostrate, surrender, and bow down in body, mind, and spirit, with all reverence, to that great Master who is dhīra, ever firm and established in the Truth, the supreme Knowledge, and the infinite Substratum of the manifest and unmanifest universe. This beautiful name is resplendent in the depth of its meaning. It points to one who is a sthitaprajña, a man of steady wisdom – the spiritual Teacher who embodies true inner strength and power arising from supreme purity and absolute knowledge.

Gurudev was courageous, fearless, calm, bold, and single-pointed in thought and action. He always remained in perfect balance and inner equipoise, untouched by the adversity of the pairs of opposites, patient and loving to all, His manner cultured and majestic, and ever of noble good conduct. Gurudev was firm and disciplined. He was the role-model of right action and correct behavior in all circumstances. He molded our character and guided us to efface the ego. At the yajñaśāla and in everyday routine, He was punctual and encouraged us to follow His example. At the same time, He was always patient, loving, and forgiving of our faults and weaknesses.

Gurudev came down from the mountains to spread the teachings of the *Bhagavad-gītā* and Upaniṣads, daring to rise above current orthodoxy and speak on the scriptures in the English language worldwide. He taught with great power and inexhaustible enthusiasm. From the podium, in satsaṅg, through His letters, and ever through His words and actions, the message of the scriptures directly reached our hearts, bringing light and removing darkness.

Gurudev lived in the present moment, actionless in all action. He declared, "Stand back and watch the flow of events in the stream of time," urging us to let go of thoughts of the past and future. He was a mirror of the Absolute, revealing to us the state of highest wisdom wherein the mind and intellect are purified and still. As the calm waters of a waveless mountain lake perfectly reflect the sun's light in the cloudless sky above, in the Master, the buddhi, totally stilled, shines forth as dhī – pure intellect. It is the instrument of inner knowing in which the Self is seen and directly experienced as one's true nature. He abided in this inner state of Self-realization and guided us unceasingly and unfailingly to realize this great Truth within ourselves.

The one who is dhīra is deep as the fathomless ocean, far away from the stormy surface, still and motionless in the expansive oneness. Gurudev lived every moment rooted in the infinite magnitude of His own being.

When our extroverted mind is stilled in devotion at the Master's feet, we are blessed by His grace to catch a 'glimpse' of His true nature. Gurudev said, "Whenever you want me, just close your eyes, look into your heart, and I will be there." Gurudev taught that the Guru is beyond the manifest physical form. In the highest sense, the Guru is our Self, limitless non-dual Consciousness, ever-guiding and supporting us on the path.

May we be ever blessed by His presence in our hearts as we chant the Holy Śrī Cinmaya Aṣṭottara Śata Nāmāvali with all reverence, devotion, and loving gratitude.

taṃ durdarśaṃ gūḍhamanupraviṣṭaṃ guhāhitaṃ gahvareṣṭhaṃ purāṇam,
adhyātmayogādhigamena devaṃ matvā dhīro harṣaśoko jahāti.

The wise sage, renounces joy and sorrow by means of meditation on the inner Self, recognizes the Ancient, who is difficult to be seen, is hidden in the cave of the heart, dwells in the abyss, is lodged in the intelligence and seated amidst miserable surroundings indeed.

~ *Kaṭhopaniṣad* 1.2.12

49

Om Dhairyapradāya Namaḥ

Salutations to the one who instills courage.

Brahmachari Dvijot Chaitanya

Reflecting on Pūjya Gurudev's journey from Rishikesh to the Himalayas to meet Swami Tapovan Maharaj, I can only conclude that Gurudev's determination for ātma-jñāna was like an unmovable mountain. No matter how difficult the journey or situation was, He didn't give up. He reached the goal. Despite knowing that walking the path of dharma is not easy, He still made a decision that would benefit all in a positive and meaningful way, showing His vision, strength, love, and understanding.

There are times when some things may seem difficult, or you may feel alone and not cared for. Yet, performing your duty and not allowing hardship to break your resolve reflects the lives of all the great saints and sages who were able to overcome difficulties and perform their duties in accordance with dharma.

Whenever I look at the grass, it reminds me of courage, that no matter the situation or condition, I should never give up or fail to do what is right. No matter how many times the grass is cut, it continues to grow, and that serves as a great reminder to keep striving for the highest, striving for freedom, to be able to live and be the absolute Truth. It also reminds me that I am in control of my situation, which makes it much easier for me to follow the path that I choose, the path to Self-realization. This is all possible due to the vision, strength, and determination that Gurudev taught us to get to know and understand who we are.

We don't always get along well or interact with one another because we think we are all different and don't know each other. But when we get to know who we truly are, that concept of being separate and different from each other goes away. Knowing that God is within you and within everything else, individuality goes away, and you love and shine without limit. Gurudev didn't just make the knowledge more accessible to us, He made sure we received it in the correct way. Pūjya Gurudev's love for us has made Him give us the best of what He got from His Guru so that we too can experience infinite Bliss. Gurudev understood the true meaning and importance of freedom and worked with great determination for us to have this freedom.

Standing up for what is right without fear is Gurudev, and that is dhairya (courage)!

In response to a devotee's fears about possible earthquakes, Pujya Gurudev wrote:
"Don't yield to such a delusory feeling. No place is safe for man! Even if California is to be drowned, you will not be the only suffering one. How are you in any way more sacred than all the others who are also the Lord's creatures?...think positively that even if such a thing happens, we will try to serve others even during our last moments. The Lord is great. Warn yourself that no place on the face of this precarious world is safe. Everywhere death can reach us. Therefore, running away from any place is not running away from death. Death is inevitable. Seek Life – the glorious source of all life – the infinite and eternal Reality."

50

Om Nārāyaṇāya Namaḥ

Salutations to the one who is Lord Viṣṇu.

Brahmachari Hari Chaitanya

In the eternal tapestry of the Advaita tradition's wisdom, there exists a profound revelation – the revelation that echoes through the ages, whispering the timeless truth: "I am That." It is not a proclamation of arrogance nor a claim of superiority but a sublime recognition of the substratum of all existence, a harmonious melody resonating through the universe.

In the heart of Advaita, the philosophy of non-duality, one discovers that the essence of every being is divine. It is an understanding that transcends the boundaries of the ego, soaring high above the realm of separateness. In this profound realization, a person can say, "I am That," not as an individual entity but as a manifestation of the universal Consciousness that permeates all things.

In the depths of Self-realization, one peels away the layers of identity, shedding the illusions of the ego, and delves into the core of being. Here, in the sacred silence of the substratum, the distinction between the self and the Divine dissolves like mist in the morning sun. The boundaries that once confined the spirit fade away, revealing an eternal Truth: the Essence within me is the Essence within all – it is the divine Essence.

To say Pūjya Gurudev is Bhagavān Nārāyaṇa in the Advaita tradition is to acknowledge the divine spark within, recognizing that the same Consciousness that breathes life into the cosmos resides within the depths of our being. It is an affirmation of our intrinsic divinity, a celebration of the unity that underlies all diversity. It is to understand that every smile, every tear, and every heartbeat is a divine expression, a dance of the cosmos manifesting through us.

In this profound understanding, the individual ego merges seamlessly with the cosmic Consciousness. The limitations of the body and mind dissolve, and a sense of boundless love, compassion, and bliss emerges. It is a state of being where the distinction between the worshiper and the worshiped vanishes, and the sacred truth dawns, recognizing the interconnectedness of all life, embracing the Divine in every being, and living in harmony with the universe.

Proclaiming Pūjya Gurudev as that Divine is not an assertion of arrogance; it is a humble acknowledgment of the ultimate Reality. It is an invitation to transcend the illusions of separateness, to dive into the ocean of oneness, and to experience the divine Presence in every moment. It is a poetic dance of the soul, echoing the eternal Truth that in the vast tapestry of existence, every thread is woven with the divine Essence.

"To a sincere devotee, nothing is impossible. Mere devotion alone is not sufficient. Devotion to the Lord must be everdancing in our heart, and our hands and legs must sweat in work, our head (intellect) must think well, and thus, 'holding on' to Him in love, let us use all the faculties and powers He has so lovingly given us. Then no one can fail. No one will lose. None can come to sorrow."
~ Swami Chinmayananda

51

Om Nijānandāya Namaḥ

Salutations to the one who is innate Bliss.

Brahmachari Soham Chaitanya

The pursuit for ānanda (happiness) is an undisputed pursuit in human life. Our scriptures discuss two types of ānanda. One comes from the material world outside (viṣaya ānanda), and the other comes from the inner world of pure consciousness (brahma ānanda). Whereas the ānanda that comes from reveling in the unbroken stream of inner bliss is nijānanda (nija ānanda).

Vedānta roars through the galleries of the Upaniṣads that our essential nature is unconditioned bliss. This bliss is effortlessly experienced every day in deep sleep. However, being ignorant, we come to identify with the body and mind and take our finite existence to be our sole identity. Just like infinite space appears to be conditioned due to the conditioning of a pot, infinite consciousness appears to be conditioned due to the conditioning of body and mind. Bhagavān Kṛṣṇa says in the *Bhagavad-gītā* that very few seekers who have gathered merits in their past births come to seek knowledge of their true Self. This quest takes them to a Guru, where they devotedly learn the scriptures, internalize it through reflection, and abide in it through meditation. Perfected wisdom reflects in them as firm abidance in the blissful Self and absence of worldly desires, due to the removal of ignorance. Such a saint is called a 'jīvanmukta' (one who is liberated while living).

Every action of such a jīvanmukta becomes a poetic expression of the ecstasy they are reveling in. They continue to live in this world and spread the fragrance of divine love wherever they go. They work in this world out of joy and not for joy. They live 'in' the world but never become 'of' the world. They demonstrate in true spirit what it means to go beyond body identification.

Once a devotee was preparing the syringe for Pūjya Gurudev's daily injection of insulin. Gurudev took the syringe and the alcohol-saturated cotton and dabbed His thigh with it, ready to give Himself an injection. The devotee found it painful to watch and turned her head away, looking outside the window.

"Why are you looking away?" enquired Gurudev.

"Gurudev, it's painful for me to watch," replied the devotee. "Doesn't it hurt you when you do it day after day?"

Gurudev's reply was simple and direct, "When I say, 'I am not the body', I am not the body!"

Our reverential salutations at the lotus feet of Pūjya Gurudev. May His grace guide us towards our Blissful Self within. "The journey is long, and alone we must walk. With love and devotion, serve all along the way. I will meet you one day – for that blissful moment, I shall wait." ~ Pūjya Gurudev Swami Chinmayananda

"Having discovered the unshakeable state of Pure Bliss within, there remains absolutely nothing in the world of names and forms that can entice or lure Him. He just goads on amongst us, fuelled by this one selfless desire to lift human Consciousness to its highest state through the teachings of Vedānta."

~ Source: Chinmaya Ashtottara Namavali, Chinmaya YouTube Channel

52

Om Nirapekṣāya Namaḥ

Salutations to the one who does not depend on anything or anyone.

Brahmachari Sudheer Chaitanya

From the highest standpoint, only those who know and experience that fullness and absoluteness can live without any expectations. This attitude leads one to come out of all dependencies. This independence results in contentment, finally leading to eternal happiness.

Pūjya Gurudev was ever independent, content, and happy. He had no expectations from anyone. Only an independent person can stay free and expect nothing, and only one who does not expect anything can be truly independent. While we may understand the concept, is it possible to practice this quality in our daily lives?

Pūjya Gurudev was nirapekṣa at both the absolute and transactional levels. He started Sandeepany Sadhanalaya in 1963 to provide the knowledge of Vedānta to all and sundry without any strings attached. People from all parts of the world, even from other spiritual organizations, study at Sandeepany Sadhanalaya without any kind of bond or binding to serve the Chinmaya Mission after the study period. The two-year course is free of cost, and everything required for the student is provided during that time, without the expectation of any gurudakṣiṇā. After the course, the students are free to choose their path as they wish.

Once, while traveling, I happened to visit a Gaṇeśā

temple in Wayanad, Kerala. I was surprised when I saw a beautiful auditorium named Swami Chinmayananda Hall on the temple premises. Upon inquiry, I learned that Pūjya Gurudev had visited the place once on His way to Mysore. He had advised and supported the temple committee in handling certain issues they were facing back then. So, as a token of gratitude, they dedicated the auditorium to Gurudev. I wonder whether Pūjya Gurudev even knew of any such auditorium named after Him!

It was natural for Gurudev to be free of expectations because fullness was His true nature and being free of expectation was sahaja (easy or natural) for Him. As seekers, we too must imbibe and practice this quality in our lives.

We often expect people to acknowledge or appreciate us for our contributions. We become sad, irritated, or even angry when we do not get the desired results, which affects our relationships. Being a member of a committee or when working with a team on projects, practicing this quality can help us grow in our spiritual life and our day-to-day life. So, whenever we are in the field to work or serve, let us keep this quality in mind and work without expectations. nirapekṣitvam at the individual level makes us content and happy, which helps us evolve. At the organizational level, we can serve society more effectively with this quality.

"Producing more than what we consume and giving more than what we take..." – should be our mantra for life!

53

Om Niḥspṛhāya Namaḥ

Salutations to the desireless one.

Brahmachari Ved Chaitanya

In Śrīmad *Bhagavad-gītā* (2.71), while painting the word-picture of a Realized Master, Lord Kṛṣṇa says:

vihāya kāmānyaḥ sarvān pumāṁścarati niḥspṛhaḥ,
nirmamo nirahaṅkāraḥ sa śāntimadhigacchati

"Having given up all desires, one who moves about free from all attachments, without the sense of 'I-ness' and 'my-ness', he attains Peace."

This verse is a depiction of the absolute state of freedom experienced by a jñānī. The important word here is 'niḥspṛhaḥ' – without any attachment. How has the jñānī attained this state of total detachment? By giving up desires, the 'my-ness', and 'I-ness'. One who has given up all his desires, ego, and attachment is said to be niḥspṛha.

Pūjya Gurudev Swami Chinmayananda was an exemplary example of this total freedom! He was a Jñānī, a Bhakta, a Vedāntī, a Sādhu, a Yogī, a Guru, and much more! We see in Him all the qualities of a sthitaprajña as explained by Lord Kṛṣṇa in the *Bhagavad-gītā*. We must reflect upon these qualities and imbibe them through practice.

The term 'spṛha' means longing for the enjoyment of sense objects. Scriptures clearly explain that to become niḥspṛha, one has to neither give up the sense-objects nor the enjoyment. What one must give up is the longing that causes the attachment to them. This longing itself transforms into desires. As Pūjya Gurudev would often say, desires at the intellectual level create thoughts at the mental level, and we act on them at the physical level. There is no end to desires. As we try to fulfill them, more desires arise, leading to more agitation, and finally to sorrow. *Manusmṛti* (2.94) says, "Never is desire appeased by the enjoyment of desire; it only waxes stronger, like fire by clarified butter." Then how to give up desires? Pūjya Gurudev gives the solution, too, "Enjoy! But without getting attached."

Once, He was sitting with a few youngsters discussing the topic of vairāgya while sipping a hot cup of coffee. Suddenly, He said, "Who says there is no joy in coffee?" There was pin-drop silence. Youngsters thought that Gurudev was contradicting Himself. If coffee gives joy, then why and how to detach from it? Their thoughts were broken when Gurudev continued, "But, it is only temporary." There is no doubt that the objects bring us joy. But that joy is only fleeting. An intelligent person keeps this in mind and enjoys the world without getting attached to that enjoyment or object. To do this, we must give up 'I-ness' – the identification with the BMI (Body-Mind-Intellect), and 'my-ness', – possessiveness with the objects of the world. Attachment arises from 'I-ness' and 'my-ness', which further creates desires, agitations, and sorrow.

Pūjya Gurudev gives a beautiful example of village women who apply oil to their hands before cutting a jackfruit. We too must apply the oil of detachment to our mind and then enjoy the world! By the grace and blessings of Pūjya Gurudev, may we too become niḥspṛha like Him!

54

Om Nirupamāya Namaḥ

Salutations to the incomparable one.

Brahmacharini Aashraya

Often, when someone is trying to explain something we have not experienced firsthand, either an example of something similar to it or a very vivid explanation is given. For instance, when explaining the northern lights, one would describe the temperature, the darkness of the night sky, the beauty when it is lit up with enchanting colors, and the sheer magical nature of it. However, when it comes to our Pūjya Gurudev, He is beyond all comparison. No example or comparison can fully encompass Him. We can try to understand Pūjya Gurudev from the standpoint of His vision and work, or Him as a teacher, or as the embodiment of the infinite Reality, however, nothing can compare to Him. In this respect, He is truly unfathomable.

Pūjya Gurudev's vision to spread the knowledge of our scriptures to people of all ages and from all walks of life is truly inspiring. His vision was such that it included all and reached far into the future, and how He meticulously worked has allowed Chinmaya Mission to continue to grow and flourish all over the world. When one starts to reflect on the number of programs and initiatives organized by Chinmaya Mission, it is truly mind-blowing. Whether ensuring access to affordable healthcare, enabling rural communities to be self-sufficient, setting up educational institutions, restoring and building temples, or bringing the ancient knowledge of our scriptures to today's contemporary world, one can only marvel at the extraordinary visionary and missionary that Pūjya Gurudev was. The vastness of His vision and the organization are a testament to Pūjya Gurudev being the unmatched one.

Aside from His unique and vast vision, Pūjya Gurudev is also widely known for His unsurpassed oration skills. Thousands of people would assemble for His jñāna-yajña, and they would be completely engrossed in His novel, hilarious and yet pointed explanations of the subtlest topics of our scriptures. Just by being in His mere presence or listening to His words, devotees' hearts would be filled with love, devotion, and clarity. Even now, when we connect with Him through His teachings, such overwhelming emotion fills our hearts.

As the Guru, Pūjya Gurudev was at times a loving parent, a strict disciplinarian, a confidante, or a guide. His love was so magnanimous that in Sandeepany Sadhanalaya, instead of the disciples going out to bring food and other resources for the Guru, He Himself went and sourced everything. He truly revolutionized the idea of a gurukula.

The Guru is none other than the Infinite. He is the very embodiment of the Infinite; thus, there is no apt comparison or example as the Infinite is One. Thus, be it Pūjya Gurudev's vision, teachings, His sense of humor, or His all-encompassing love, there is truly no comparison. However, when we turn our mind to even one aspect of such a One, the mind becomes silent and, in turn, is filled with reverence, awe, wonder, love, and surrender. Thus, we come to know Pūjya Gurudev – the Incomparable One!

55

Om Nirvikalpāya Namah

Salutations to the one who is ever undisturbed.

Jaya Muzumdar

Is it possible to remain without thoughts?

The mind is a flow of thoughts, so to remain without thoughts would mean to be without the mind. Is this a mindless state that describes Pūjya Gurudev, or was His a thought-free state of the mind? What does it mean to be 'thought-free'? Why should we try to be 'thought-free'?

If we look at our lives, we find that our mind is the one that persecutes us the most. *Amṛtabindu-upaniṣad* declares that the mind is the cause of our bondage as well as liberation.

In the sixth chapter of the *Bhagavad-gītā*, Śrī Kṛṣṇa tells us to lift ourselves by ourselves and advises us to befriend our minds. A friend encourages us to remain on the right path and is quick to stop us from pursuing a wrong action. When the mind is under the complete control of the intellect, it is our friend, but if it goes outside with the senses, it becomes our enemy – one that troubles and persecutes us and does not desire our well-being. If we are unable to befriend our mind, it will drag us outside and take us further away from our goal of liberation, as is stated in the scriptures.

So, if we have to make the mind our friend, we need to understand and know it first. We know that we cannot be the mind because when we are in the deep sleep state, we forget our worries and anxieties and are very peaceful. This peaceful state can and should be achieved while also in the waking state. The mind will then become our friend and the cause of our liberation. Pūjya Gurudev, having known this, transcended the mind and realized His own Self as being the Self in all.

Mind is of the nature of saṅkalpa-vikalpa. It oscillates between what we 'want' to do and what we 'ought' to do. If we merely do what we want to do, then chances are it is dragging us away from our goal, which could be spiritual or secular. But if we do what we are supposed to do, then the mind is our friend and is taking us towards our goal. At any given moment, when the mind doesn't oscillate and makes the right choices, quick and correct decisions are possible. The mind can achieve a thought-free state, free of agitations and persecutions. When the mind is free from the oscillations of 'to do or not to do', it is one with the intellect and knows exactly what needs to be done at any given moment. This state can be achieved by keeping the mind always under the control of the intellect and using it as an instrument, to be used as and when we need it, as we want it to behave.

Pūjya Gurudev, using the mind and intellect as His instruments while making any and all decisions, always remained in a state of nirvikalpa. This state is free of thoughts and at peace, no matter what the situation outside! If we can achieve this, we can be considered to be in a state of nirvikalpa or the 'thought-free' state of mind that Pūjya Gurudev enjoyed!

56

Om Nityāya Namaḥ

Salutations to the Eternal One.

Gina Singh

As a young CHYK (Chinmaya Yuva Kendra), whenever I would listen to stories of devotees and disciples who met and spent time with Pūjya Gurudev, I often envied them and wished that I, too, had the opportunity to meet Him, receive personal letters from Him, hear His thundering voice and feel His infinite love. Alas, I was born a little too late!

That envy was futile, that wish was unnecessary, and that understanding was incomplete because Pūjya Gurudev is not away from us even today. He never was and never will be. He truly is Eternal, and His presence can be felt, seen, and experienced everywhere by everyone, and at all times in the universe.

Pūjya Gurudev knew He was Eternal, even though His body was perishing. Having realized His eternal Nature, He dedicated His life to ensuring that we too realize that we are Eternal and that there is no separation between us and Him.

His instructions to countless seekers echo similar sentiments, perhaps with the hope that our dull-witted minds will be inspired to become aware of His eternal presence and our eternal nature.

For those still looking to find Him:

- His words are eternal; we meet Him through the words of His disciples, books, lectures, and letters.
- His legacy is eternal; Pūjya Guruji once said, "We

have seen what Chinmaya has done. Now we will see what His name will do." We are seeing a snowball effect of the selfless work of Gurudev and the positive contribution to society that graduates of Bala Vihar are making by being good citizens of the world!

- His vision is eternal; understanding the need for the lost knowledge of our ṛṣis in our daily lives, Gurudev dedicated His life to transforming not just our lives but also our visions. Chinmaya will always remain synonymous with the spiritual revival of Sanātana Dharma in the 21st century when it was most needed. He inspired thousands to selflessly serve society through Chinmaya Mission and beyond.
- His promise is eternal; Gurudev says to spiritual seekers in His *Kaṭhopaniṣad* commentary – "Be optimistic; and if you cannot, each of you may take it from Chinmaya: Thou art a fit adhikārī, and with a little self-effort thou shalt reach, in this very birth, the Supreme and the Godly achievement. Never hesitate. Never doubt, but sincerely strive and achieve."
- His Love is eternal; "Look into your heart, and you shall find me there" were Gurudev's final words!
- He is Eternal; He is the very Self, the Consciousness that forms the substratum of this entire universe.

Blessed are we to have a Guru who is not only Eternal but whose eternal vision is to ensure that we realize we, too, are Eternal.

57

Om Nirañjanāya Namaḥ

Salutations to the taintless one.

Swami Atmavidananda

Our ancient ṛṣis found many methods to make the student understand the Truth (satyam), which is to be experienced in sādhana. One of those methods is understanding the Unknown through the known.

Many a time, our ṛṣi paraṁparā described the supreme Consciousness as nirañjanam. The etymological meaning of the word nirañjanam is nirgatam añjanam yasyaḥ saḥ nirañjanam. Nirgatam – without any; añjanam – dark or black spot. The word añjanam is always referred to in scriptures as ignorance. The word nirañjanam has multiple meanings, like pure, spotless, impeccable, and without any material contamination. Thus, the actual meaning of nirañjanāya is – the one who revels in the knowledge of supreme Consciousness devoid of worldly ignorance.

This supreme Reality, Satyam, is always beyond all worldly contaminations like names and forms, which are the products of ignorance. Pūjya Gurudev lived in such a Reality till His last breath. Pūjya Gurudev is none other than the manifestation of that supreme Reality – Brahman. Because He is nirañjanam, one can feel the great quality reflected in His teachings, writings, leadership, and organizational abilities. And at the same time, He always remained untouched by all the worldly impurities.

This nirañjana sthiti is His strength and power, expressed

in His walk and talk everywhere. As a Master and visionary, He was always clear with His ideology, which made Him fearless. Whenever I sat close to Pūjya Gurudev, I truly felt that serene vibration emanating from His nirañjana sthiti.

In December 1990, Chinmaya Mission, Vijayawada, organized a press-meet with Pūjya Gurudev. Nearly twenty senior journalists from local and national print media attended that meeting. They were all ready with many questions for Him. Slowly, Gurudev came and sat in His chair facing all the press people. Suddenly, He started His talk, roaring like a lion about the need for Ayodhya Ram Mandir, a burning issue of those times. For almost forty-five minutes, He spoke, and before stopping His speech, He asked, looking at all the journalists, "Any questions?" The entire group of journalists and all the visitors were mesmerized and remained in absolute silence. After one minute, a columnist from Indian Express got up and said humbly, "Swamiji, your ideas are spotless. That's why we are all speechless. In one shot, you answered all our questions without any need for questioning." He could make the outer world speechless with His inner quality of spotless knowledge.

Nirañjanam is neither a noun nor a verb. It is the nature of that supreme Ātman (ātma-lakṣaṇa), which is to be contemplated and meditated upon. And it is a state to be attained and experienced.

One who attains and revels in such nirvikalpa nirañjana sthiti will remain as jīvanmukta forever. I have always felt blessed to have seen and traveled with such a great Mahātmā. I offer my humble prostrations at the holy feet of such a personification of śuddha Ātman.

58

Om Paramāya Namaḥ

Salutations to the Supreme.

Brahmacharini Jyoti Chaitanya

The superlatives of Sanskrit grammar are a group of adjectives used to describe an entity that lies unsurpassed in its caliber. In every way, Supreme.

alabdhvātiśayam yasmād - vyāvruttāstamabādayaḥ,
garīyase namastasmā avidyāgranthibhedine.

"Salutations to that Supreme Guru who breaks the knot of ignorance (in the heart of His disciples). The superlatives, having found no more worthy a recipient, have returned to alight on this One, (My Guru), the embodiment of the Supreme." (Naiśkarmyasiddhi 1.2)

In this inspiring verse, Śrī Sureśvarācārya poetically expresses that the superlatives, having searched the entire creation to discover a being who could personify the excellence of their essence, could find none who excelled the caliber of his Guru, Śrī Ādi Śankarācārya, and so they relinquished their titles of supremacy upon this epitome of perfection, the Guru.

Our Pūjya Gurudev, Swami Chinmayananda, was indeed an embodiment of that same supreme perfection described by Śrī Sureśvarācārya – a peerless Guru who was 'param':

- Supreme in His knowledge (of all scriptures past)

- Supreme in His conduct (in all circumstances present)
- Supreme in His vision and mission (for the future)

As with those of truly supreme Nature, their defining feature has always been the uniqueness of their thoughts and the monumental expansivity of their vision. True to this, our Pūjya Gurudev was known for offering the most unexpected but visionary of answers to the most seemingly simple questions. This allowed His awestruck listeners a glimpse into a mind that was truly rooted in the 'param', the Highest Truth. Such instances were too numerous to count, but a brief recount of just a few would suffice to inspire.

Gurudev would use ironic aphorisms to tease the agile mind of the youth that would both bemuse and amuse, as He instructed them, "Be aggressively good! But to do so, hasten slowly." When conversing with householder sādhakas, He would caution on the distinction between freedom and licentiousness, offering the seemingly contradictory quip, "Remember! Freedom is the ability to NOT do what you want to do."

But most magnificently, whether sporting with devotees or supporting them through challenges, the gems of His superior wisdom would shine like the stars, even as He references these celestials themselves, saying, "Understand that peace is not the absence of afflictions, but feeling the presence of God within, even during them. God's presence is like the stars – the darker the night, the brighter they shine!... we cannot piece together the puzzle of our lives; remember, the best view is from above! Let us allow Him to put us together, as His guidance alone is ever perfect and unerring."

59

Om Parabrahmaṇe Namaḥ

Salutations to Him, who is Absolute Reality.

Brahmacharini Kritika Chaitanya

Pūjya Gurudev indicated in His teachings that our true nature is Parabrahma – Supreme, Divine, Infinite, Absolute – that encompasses the totality of all existence. I 'am' pure Existence, not the existence 'of' a thing. But we mistake ourselves to be finite and thus identify with the limited and react to the ups and downs of our everyday interactions as though they are real and true. We do not really see any object, person, place, or experience in totality; we see only our own limited, preconceived notions about it. One minute, we love the hot sun, but we dislike it the next minute. When the rains finally cool us down, we complain that it is gloomy.

The universe continues to change, as do our experiences and our knowledge of it. All things are constantly in a flux, but the 'is-ness' that supports all things is that Parabrahman. It is all things in the universe; It is that which sustains all things, and in It, all things manifest from one form to another. It is from where our experiences arise and where all our experiences occur. Therefore, Parabrahman is beyond omniscient, omnipotent, and omnipresent. It is not just omniscient; all knowledge is Parabrahman. It is not just omnipotent; Parabrahman is power itself. It is not just omnipresent, but presence exists within Parabrahman.

Pūjya Gurudev, through His work and teachings, keeps us thinking about our source, course, and ultimate goal. He taught that whatever we are experiencing is the pure, infinite Reality. That alone Is, and we are that absolute Reality and should not be shaken by the ever-changing, trivial things in life. Pūjya Gurudev says, "I am being. I am not an experience; I allow the experiences to exist around me." We should remember that we are not limited by our instruments and faculties but that we are the very notion of limitlessness. I am that supreme Brahman; I allow experiences to exist in me. I am not the experience. I am the same as all things subtle and gross within and without me, yet my limited intellect cannot begin to fathom this! But Pūjya Gurudev joyfully taught repeatedly that we are one and the same. He asked, "You think you came to the universe? From where? Think! Or did the universe manifest you?" He interacted with sādhakas from the level of the supreme Self: "I promise I will not leave you. If I leave you, where is 'you'? I am the very 'Sat' (Existence)."

When someone is able to perform a task easily, admirably, and with grace, we say it is like their 'second nature'. But we do not 'consider' Pūjya Gurudev's mahimā to be 'second nature'; we 'know', whether or not we realize it, that it is His very nature. Pūjya Gurudev's Ānanda remained unbroken because He realized the very nature of the supreme Reality – Sat-Cit-Ānanda, the source of eternal joy. He relayed the highest Knowledge with such love and clarity over and over again, through words and actions, and allowed us a glimpse of our supreme Nature – Parabrahman. If we are able to reflect and practice His teachings, reflect on His simple yet extraordinary life, then slowly we can reach that Truth.

60

Om Pāvanāya Namaḥ

Salutations to the one who is pure.

Brahmacharini Shripriya Chaitanya

Every seeker, in order to attain their goal, must become what they are seeking. Spiritual students seeking the Truth, practice being truthful in their actions, speech, and thoughts. That same Truth is indicated as 'pure' (pāvana), and it is with that in mind we offer our prostrations to Pūjya Gurudev.

For a Self-realized Master, there can be no question of his purity or impurity. Impurity implies the taint of another substance, and the saint is one who knows himself to be nothing but the one non-dual Truth. For him, there is nothing other than the Self and nothing to bring impurity. Thus, there can be no question of purity because there is no second entity. He is pure because He alone is.

Nevertheless, spiritual seekers of Truth strive towards purity as a matter of priority in their quest for perfection. The dust and dirt that accumulates around worldly objects, including the seeker's own body, can be washed away. The seeker seeks purity for the mind since its ability to function free from bias paves the way towards Self-knowledge. How can the mind be impure?

The mind has two aspects: one which belongs to the world and the other to the Truth. When the world begins to sway over our mind, thereby curbing its freedom, we seek to free it from those undue influences and make it pure. But the mind cannot function in a vacuum, so if we seek to reduce thoughts centered on objects of the world, where should they be directed? To that which is pure by nature: to the Master, at whose feet the inspiration to strive for Truth has come to us, and by whose guidance and teachings we attain our own Self. He is pure, and by immersing our minds in Him, we draw closer to the Truth that He is.

Pāvana indicates not only that which is pure but also that by which all the purifiers and great forces of the world function. In the Viṣṇusahasranāma, Bhagavān is not only the air (pavana) that purifies but that which enlivens the air (pāvana). The *Taittirīya-upaniṣad* (2.8.1) declares, "Through fear of Him the wind blows. Through fear of Him rises the sun. Through fear of Him runs fire, Indra, and death, the fifth." Everything in nature has a unique function, but everything functions in a regulated, governed manner. The Supreme Being is pointed out as the unseen guiding hand, and because of this, every aspect of the universe is empowered to perform its prescribed role.

As seekers of Truth and disciples of the Master, we must recognize that we do not work in this world by our own power. Whether we strive for material gain or spiritual progress, we do so because we have been given the gift of life and the ability to think and act. When we see Him as That because of which we have these gifts, every action can become a dedication at His lotus feet. Not only are we bereft of life without Him, but He is our means to purification and our goal, that which is pure by nature. May we remain ever at His feet!

tadejati tannaijati taddūre tadvantike,
tadantarasya sarvasya tadu sarvasyāsya bāhyataḥ.

The Atman moves and It moves not; It is far and It is near; It is within all this, and It is also outside all this.

~ *Īśāvāsya-upaniṣad* 5

61

Om Pāvakāya Namaḥ

Salutations to the one who purifies.

Brahmacharini Shubhani Chaitanya

A seeker's only dharma in life is to realize the Truth. In order to do so, one needs a pure mind – a mind in which sattva dominates, where rajas and tamas are overpowered so that knowledge can shine forth. The one who can guide us and lead us to this purity of mind is pāvaka, or the purifier. Our pāvaka is Pūjya Gurudev, Swami Chinmayananda.

When we reflect upon His life, we see how He inspired us to purify ourselves at all levels. The glory of a saint is their ability to relate to people of various ages, backgrounds, and walks of life. Gurudev showed every one of us a unique way to purify ourselves, be it children, youth, adults, or seekers.

Gurudev inspired the founding of Bala Vihar and emphasized sharing meaningful stories of our religion with children in a vibrant way. He even wrote an extensive article on *Bāla Rāmāyaṇā* that reminds us to 'tell' and never teach a story. "To bring the story of Rāmāyaṇā to our growing children at home is the best education that parents can give to their sons and daughters – an education that can instill into them a reverence for life, a sense of moral beauty and spiritual alertness."

For the youth, He inspired the founding of CHYK (Chinmaya Yuva Kendra) with the motto: 'Harnessing youth potential through dynamic spirituality'. By engaging youth in creative projects, He gave them an outlet to express their talents and channelize them towards a higher purpose. He also encouraged youth to aim high and go beyond their body identification through selfless work. In *Bhaja Govindam*, a favorite text among youth, He writes, "To spend one's entire lifetime in sheer body-worship, in earning more so that this futile worship may be made more elaborate, is one of the abominable intellectual stupidities into which humanity readily sinks."

He inspired the purification of the minds of adults by initiating systematic study groups starting from *Kindle Life* or *Self-Unfoldment*. On the topic of introspection, Gurudev gives an example of a dead rat. If we knew that there was a dead rat in our closet, would we leave it there? Similarly, if we become aware of negative traits in us, can we disregard them without wanting to make a change? His formula of IDNS – Introspect, Detect, Negate, and Substitute – is a very effective tool for all of us to remove impurities from our minds.

The realization of the Self does not happen from just listening to the scriptures. It requires us to continuously work on ourselves, to truly be equanimous amidst failure and success, honor and dishonor, joy and sorrow. To facilitate this, Gurudev provided a field of service to all seekers – teaching, community outreach, rural development, and more. This field is an immense blessing that gives us an opportunity to purify further; it shatters our ego and teaches us complete surrender to the Infinite. It also allows us to serve alongside seekers and learn from their wisdom and experience.

Above and beyond this, Gurudev gave us the most purifying gift, the knowledge of the Self. Upon developing such a pure mind, He then asks us to transcend it – for we are ever pure as Brahman, the Self. Salutations to the one who purifies us to great heights so we can realize that we are ever, as pure as the Self.

62

Om Puruṣōttamāya Namaḥ

Salutations to the most uplifted being.

Brahmacharini Shweta Chaitanya

As vedāntins, we may see this word and immediately think of the Upaniṣadik puruṣa, the innate essence of all creation, the One without a second, the ultimate Truth, and the true Self of all. The Guru paramparā tradition beautifully reminds us that our spiritual teachers are an expression of this puruṣa. So, as students, we look upon our Gurus as representations of the ultimate teaching of the Self.

This meaning certainly comes to mind when I think of Pūjya Gurudev Swami Chinmayananda. Still, I'm moved by how He effortlessly embodied this lofty word as a guide among us. Without hesitation, Gurudev opened the doors to the sacred teachings of Advaita Vedānta to all people, breaking barriers of caste, gender, occupation, and all other identity markers that once barred so many from accessing these teachings. His numerous talks and translations offer an impactful perspective on Advaita, opening up possibilities for people from all walks of life. To make skillful changes, especially in a space where tradition is largely untouched, it takes a master in wisdom and a knower of hearts – a true puruṣottama. The best or 'uttama' is rarely ever run of the mill. It stands out, leaves an impression, stays in our minds, and is different from the rest. Just think of your favorite food, or book, or memory.

Pūjya Gurudev strikes me as different because He cared deeply for the upliftment of everyone who sought this knowledge during His time and for generations to come. Sādhana can feel and seem like a solo journey, and it is to a certain extent, but Gurudev's actions remind us that to see the Self in ourselves, we must learn to acknowledge, honor, and care for that same Self in the world around us. The Self is, after all, shining brightly in a shared creation.

I never had the good fortune of meeting Pūjya Gurudev, but I am a product of His vision to create an inclusive space for seekers of Advaita far and wide.

O Gurudev!
Release me if you would
I cannot sustain in sorrow
"Tomorrow"
Alas, tomorrow I may be in joy
and foolishly deny release
So delay not, deny not
Your grace, my freedom.

~ A short poem by Swamini Vimalananda written in the year1984.

63

Om Prasannātmane Namaḥ

Salutations to the cheerful one.

Brahmacharini Stuti Chaitanya

In 1970, Pūjya Gurudev had a heart attack when He was in Mysore. Many people came to the hospital to visit Him. He always maintained a jovial mood and would joke about the inconveniences He had to put up with. Someone noticed a bedbug and flicked it away. "Isn't that my luck? Lord Viṣṇu is sleeping on that wonderful snake in the milky ocean, and all I get are a few stray bugs!" Pūjya Gurudev jested.

What does it mean to be cheerful? Pūjya Gurudev encapsulates, "The greatest joy is not to have any cause for sorrow or pain. The greatest wealth is to feel content with what one has. A content life sparkles with joy." In the same way, courage is not the absence of fear; cheerfulness is not the absence of pain, suffering, anxiety, and so on. Genuine happiness arises from a sense of fulfillment – physical strength, mental poise, intellectual acumen, and, most importantly, spiritual perfection. This feeling of completeness is holistic in nature.

Just as the physical body requires sustenance and maintenance, the mind, intellect, and spiritual aspects of our personalities also need regular nourishment and nurturing for us to feel like wholesome beings. Pūjya Gurudev instructs, "The greatest joy in life is giving, loving, and sacrificing. To give, we must have abundance in ourselves. We can't give what we have not. Therefore, first, create fullness."

Chāndogya-upaniṣad declares, "yo vai bhūmā tatsukham" – That which is indeed the Infinite, That is joy.

If we want to take care of the physical instrument, the body, we proceed to the kitchen and the gym. Where do we turn for the tuning of the inner instrument? If we are to flourish in our spiritual quest, we have no other alternative but to gain mastery over the fickle mind. Indeed, we should visit the satsaṅg halls frequently to vitalize the inner instrument. There, we learn the source of joy and how we, too, can develop this sense of fulfillment.

In the *Bhagavad-gītā*, Bhagavān Śri Kṛṣṇa proclaims to Arjuna, "This whole world is pervaded by Me in My unmanifest form." With this revelation, our mind-intellect shifts attention to the Lord of our hearts as the substratum of the entire creation.

When we are able to focus single-pointedly on the glorious divinity pulsating throughout the universe, our hearts become full and overflowing with unconditional love. The inner instrument rhythmically dances in ecstasy and sings in jubilance. Joy is, therefore, a reflection of the divinity present within.

The next phase of our sādhana is understanding I am that source of joy. Ānanda is not a quality that can be cultivated; rather, we must live in the awareness that 'I am ānanda-svarūpa ātmā'. With the grace and blessings of Bhagavān, our sādhana is to develop this understanding through regular satsaṅg (śravaṇam), meticulous reflection (mananam), and constant remembrance (nididhyāsanam) of this precious knowledge imparted by the Guru. Through these means, the knowledge will naturally be expressed in our daily lives as prasannatā (cheerfulness).

64

Om Phalāsakti-rahitāya Namaḥ

Salutations to the one who is free from attachments to the fruits of action.

Brahmacharini Taarini Chaitanya

"Success is in the race run and not the trophy won." This oft-used quote by Pūjya Gurudev Swami Chinmayananda might seem simple to the eye yet is potent with promise for one who can understand the wisdom therein and practice it.

"If success is what you seek, then never strive with a mind dissipated with anxieties and fears for the fruit" – so the scriptures proclaim. An action performed in the present, when tethered to a future moment, materializes as the fruit of that action. In essence, an action's rewards are inseparable from the action itself. Therefore, to obsess over and be preoccupied with anxieties regarding the rewards of our actions is to forsake the present moment, choosing instead to dwell in an unborn future. Thus, the Lord advises us not to waste the present moment in fruitless dreams and fears but to bring our best to the present and live every moment to the fullest. Dedicating the action to the higher brings out the best in us making us forget ourselves in the action. Such inspired action itself is our reward!

The one who can relinquish attachment to the fruits of actions and be centered in the Truth with a steady intellect is not swayed by circumstances, good or bad. Gurudev says that such a person becomes the instrument of knowing Brahman, and one who knows Brahman verily becomes Brahman. Such a person no longer works for happiness but operates from happiness!

In a letter in the early 1950s, addressing the committee members as 'Soldiers of the Renaissance Army', Pūjya Gurudev writes about the attitude in which a jñāna yajña should be organized so that it enables personal growth and spiritual maturity. "Renounce all anxieties. Meet each devotee and explain the work we are doing, ask for their cooperation and help – and watch. Even when you get a refusal to help from individuals, watch on in perfect detachment to see Him talking through that individual. Smile at refusals; smile at those who offer help; all activities are His play. See Nārāyaṇā's expressions everywhere. Success is ours if we know how to work in surrender unto Him, for He knows no failure ever! More than the satisfaction of the successful yajña is the joy of seeing our friends steadily growing in their spiritual stature. Remember, balance in joy and sorrow, equipoise in mind and intellect, and general cheer in yourself and others coming near you, are the signs of growth. Grow. Grow."

Indeed, Pūjya Gurudev is the personification of that perfect yogī who lived a life full of activity, serving all at all times, but keeping Himself as a spectator of all happenings. Even now, three decades after He left His mortal frame, we experience His vision at work – taking shape through myriad activities and projects. Devotees recollect how after bhikṣā, Gurudev would playfully pick fruits from the fruit basket and throw them out at the devotees sitting in front of Him, and when He threw the last fruit, He would dust off His hands and say, "Karma-phala is over!" In Gurudev's words, "The realized saint is not responsible for what He is doing. He is one with life. And life expresses itself in action."

65

Om Bahubhaktāya Namaḥ

Salutations to the one with many devotees.

Brahmacharini Divya

"A sannyāsī's only work is to be in samādhi. He must remain in his humble kuṭiyā! Why do you come to the towns and cities? Go back to your kuṭiyā in the Himalayas!

Priya Ātman, immortal Self!...To send them back to their kuṭiyās, there is only one method: be thyself perfect. Get out of the saṁsārik mire. Wipe your face clean. Spread cheerful smiles of joy where today there are ugly tears of sorrow! – and the Mahātma goes back to the kuṭiyā, but not till then!!

Yet, sympathetically understanding the general import of your letter, Chinmaya answers your doubt. A sannyāsī among the masses trying to bless the generation through seva is doing only a fraction of what he could bring about by the spiritual waves of divine influence generated during his hours of meditation. Yet, priya Sowmya, the sādhu in meditation, is only one part of the whole. The ulcerated world has to be taught how to empower their seriously affected heads and hearts to the curative spiritual rays of the Himalayas. This is the exclusive job of the specialists – the sannyāsins. Chinmaya is down amidst you, only to help you, to serve you, and to save you.

Once you have learned the art of living the 'Inner Life of Perfection', you shall become the powerful receiver that you really are. Then, Chinmaya shall go back to meditate and pray for the saṁsārins and the saṁsār." (Vedanta Through Letters)

Before leaving the Himalayas, Pūjya Gurudev, contemplated over this formidable challenge of "facing the educated class of India and bringing to their faithless hearts, at least a ray of understanding of what our wondrous culture stands for. Watching Mother Ganga Devī in her incessant hurry, I seemed to hear the words interlaced in her roar, 'Son, don't you see me; born here in the Himalayas, I rush down to the plains, taking with me both life and nourishment to all in my path. Fulfillment of any possession is in sharing it with others.' I felt encouraged, I felt reinforced. The urge became irresistible!" (*Journey of the Master*)

He rushed forth to nourish the average drowning saṃsārin with the anchors of Vedānta philosophy. Starting with just four attendees in a Ganeśa temple in Pune, it swelled and spread over forty years to over 500 Chinmaya Mission centers worldwide.

His schedule included two to three public lectures a day, visiting a new city every few weeks, and eventually becoming a globetrotter, with thousands of letters following His ever-moving desk. Devi groups and adult study groups were started. Bala Vihar and Yuva Kendra educated and ignited the dynamism in the country's youth. Every program, every discourse, every book, and every letter became the precious prasād that generations would be blessed with.

Pūjya Swami Chinmayananda brought out the best in everyone, no matter their beliefs or way of life. Their initial spark of interest transformed into Guru bhakti. Bhakti for the Guru builds the firm bridge of bhakti to Bhagavān. This beautiful relationship is a profound and transformative spiritual connection that transcends ordinary love and leads us back to the kuṭiyā of our Divine Nature.

66

Om Bandha-mocakāya Namaḥ

Salutations to the one who is liberated from bondage.

Swamini Vimalananda

Anything that restricts or limits us physically (aging in time) and psychologically (ignorance) is a cause of bondage (bandhaka). The resultant sorrow, frustration, anger, stress, tension, helplessness, doubts, conflicts, confusion, fear, and so on, is the feeling of bondage (bandhana). Our likes and dislikes, compulsions and attachments, desires and desire-prompted actions are all bandhakas and bandhanas. Troubled by them, we cry out to God in helplessness. It is His infinite grace that brings into our life, a Realized Master like Pūjya Gurudev.

Pūjya Gurudev's presence, His penetrating look, smile and laughter, His loving touch and casual words, a joke shared and a remark, or a fruit (prasād) or advice given by Him, dispelled our doubts, stress, and sorrow, and filled us with peace and joy. A devotee who had been through a harrowing relationship found great solace in Pūjya Gurudev's words, "No person in the world is worth your precious tears." Om bandha-mocakāya namaḥ – Salutations to Pūjya Gurudev, who gave succor, solace, and relief to those suffering from worldly afflictions.

He founded a mission that allows us to serve, learn, and transform, whereby we are rid of our likes and dislikes, pride, prejudice, pettiness, and selfishness. Om bandha-mocakāya namaḥ – Salutations to Pūjya Gurudev, whose vision and mission help us rid of all obstacles in our spiritual journey.

The Guru outside connects us to the Guru within. The Guru outside is a person with a personality. The inner Guru is knowledge. The Guru manifests at subtler and subtler levels as we progress spiritually. Initially, he gives the understanding of life and the solutions to worldly problems and removes attachments and false notions. Thereafter, he takes the form of understanding of the Self/Truth and its firm determination. The ultimate Guru is the mature knowledge thought (brahmākāra vṛtti) that removes ignorance, the ultimate Liberation. Om bandha-mocakāya namaḥ – Salutations to Pūjya Gurudev, who bestows Liberation.

Initially, within us, the Guru is a caring witness to our immaturity (upadraṣṭā). As we become open to grace, he becomes an encourager and supporter (anumantā). As we start living the life of a seeker, he becomes a nourisher of all our endeavors (bhartā). When we start enjoying a truly spiritual life, he revels with us (bhoktā). As we surrender more and more, he takes charge of our life (Maheśvara). Ultimately, in Liberation, we realize him as the supreme Self/Truth within (Paramātmā) (*Bhagavad-gītā* 13.22). Pūjya Gurudev fulfills all these roles in our life.

Om bandha-mocakāya namaḥ – Salutations to Pūjya Gurudev, who bestows Liberation wherein we realize that He is our own Self.

His life, work, and teachings did and will continue to liberate mankind for centuries to come. Om bandha-mocakāya namaḥ – Salutations again and again to Pūjya Gurudev, the yuga puruṣa who liberates us from all bondages!

67

Om Brahmaniṣṭhāya Namaḥ

Salutations to the one who is firmly established in Brahman.

Brahmacharini Akalka

Brahman is nameless, formless, without parts, and indescribable. Brahman is beyond the material realm of time, object, space, modification, growth, and loss. In fact, the Upaniṣads (*Bṛhadāraṇyaka-upaniṣad* 2.3.6) declare the Self as neti neti (not this, not this). Whatever can be within the ambit of words and ideas, the Reality is other than that. Words turn helplessly away from This (yato vāco nivartante – *Taittirīya-upaniṣad* 2.9).

When the description is only in terms of indescribability, what to say of the Master who walks as Brahman, talks as Brahman, exists as the Self, yet remains established as the infinite Existence-Consciousness-Bliss, beyond all physical and metaphysical expression? The Master who speaks to us, laughs with us, tirelessly and compassionately shows us the ever-fresh and ever-green path! What description can be applied to such a one?

At the lotus feet of the great ṛṣis, as students, we sit with minds full of doubts and confusion, and we wonder. How can this package of physical and subtle matter we are so identified with be an illusion? Can it be because our true Self is the Reality, ever unattached and free?

In Pūjya Gurudev, this nameless, formless, unmanifest Truth manifested. In the entire boundless cosmos, we see the only real wonder of wonders – a 'logical' impossibility in full and glorious expression. The formless playing in the world of form and at the same time being untouched by all limitations of form!

Many blessed bhaktas walked with Pūjya Gurudev, sat with Him, and soaked in His presence in every possible arena. Roaring like a lion, laughing with and gently guiding curious seekers, teasing dear ones, heartily eating sumptuous bhikṣā prepared by loving hands, Gurudev shook away the countless lifetimes of tamasik stupor of blessed bhaktas. Like Arjuna (*Bhagavad-gītā* 11.41, 42), we wonder – O Lord, I sat beside You, ate beside You, perhaps cracked playful jokes with You – the immeasurable, immortal, and infinite! Sitting beside and seeing You, perhaps even for days or weeks at a time, and over the years, I truly did not see You. Why? Because I tried to see You with my eyes, hear You with my ears, speak to You with words. But I could not discover You there. I am lost in the deepest well of ignorance and confusion, wholly dependent on You; where can I meet You?

The very signature of Pūjya Gurudev can tell us. "Thy Own Self, Chinmaya," reads the bold strokes of Pūjya Gurudev's pen in the closing of many of His letters. In trying to see Him outside, we are like the bird attempting to interact with its reflection in the mirrored glass. We reach out with our senses toward the reflection of our own Self in the form of our beloved Guru. But only when we look within do we find the summation and summit of our seeking. Brahmaniṣṭhā – established in Brahman, rooted in Self, fixed in the Truth – this is the place we meet Pūjya Gurudev, in our heart of hearts, unchanging, self-luminous, self-effulgent and ever-free, our very own Self. Salutations to Him!

68

Om Brahmaparāya Namaḥ

Salutations to the one for whom Brahman alone is Supreme.

Swami Sivayogananda

Most people consider the worldly objects or achievements as supreme. They are 'viṣaya-paraḥ'. Children may consider their playthings as supreme. Others may consider wealth, knowledge, or fame as supreme. In short, whatever gives happiness in line with one's desires is considered supreme. However, even after a particular desire is fulfilled, the satisfaction and happiness derived from these material objects do not last forever because those objects satisfy only a small fraction of the desires nurtured. There are so many unfulfilled desires in the form of vāsanās, and the force of these pulsating vāsanās constantly pushes a person to seek one object after another restlessly. How can such ephemeral pleasures be considered as ultimate?

On the other hand, the person who derives happiness or bliss from Brahman stays content forever and seeks nothing thereafter. This is so because the bliss of Brahman is not due to the fruition of desires or vāsanās, but in contrast, it blossoms from the elimination of all desires and vāsanās in the effulgent light of Self-knowledge. Hence, abidance in Brahman alone is ultimate.

Therefore, everyone must first precisely define the meaning of 'supreme' in their lives. There is no doubt that objects of this world do offer pleasure. Vedānta does not discount it. It only cautions us not to falsely consider them as ultimate. Vedānta advises us to wisely use these worldly engagements as stepping stones, to purify and raise ourselves closer to that which is truly Supreme, and then to abide in it permanently.

Brahman is considered Supreme because It is the substratum of everything that is manifest. Nothing transcends It. It is not opposed to anything. It is the light of all lights that transcends both light and darkness. This all-encompassing Truth accepts everything and rejects nothing. This Truth continuously and spontaneously manifests in and through all thoughts and actions of those who have realized It.

Pūjya Gurudev was an exemplar of constant residence in this Truth. He was equally at ease while acting in the world as when He was in quietude. Action never took Him away from the Source. Even in the midst of all activity, His attention never swerved from the Truth. His actions always carried the fragrance of Brahman, which was felt by all who came into His fold. This fragrance continues to spread even today.

It is indeed true that the real meaning of what Brahman is, which may appear abstract to most, can be truly understood only through the lives lived by great jñānīs like Pūjya Gurudev. He showed us all how to live in the light of that Brahman. As the *Bhagavad-gītā* says – anchoring all actions in the Truth, being inseparably yoked to It, ever contemplating on It as the One Supreme, Pūjya Gurudev worked in this world and taught others to follow the same. Hence, this salutation – brahmaparāya namaḥ – truly befits Him and shines as a gem in His crown.

69

Om Bhayanāśanāya Namaḥ

Salutations to the one who is the destroyer of fear.

Aroona Kanhai

In life, regardless of age, gender, religion, and any other apparent difference, all beings pursue the same goal: happiness! Yet we are hindered by our expectations, desires, anxieties, and fears, which dwell within our hearts, immobilizing us from achieving this elusive goal.

From the gross to the subtle, fear (bhayam) manifests in countless ways, including losing our loved ones, possessions, memories, intelligence, and even our own lives. Therefore, modern therapeutic practices have devised a number of methods to manage fear. We may just learn to live with it, ignoring it when we can, yet inevitably, it rises at some point, until eventually, the fear that we hid from weakens us, leaving us feeling hopeless and helpless. Among all the things we fear, the greatest is that of the unknown; the very root of that fear is our ignorance.

If we study the lives of the great Mahātmās, we see many examples of fearless living. Those great ones dared to step away from the comfort zones we all have become so attached to. With the power of their resolve, the discipline of sādhana, and the trust in those who have walked the path before, they lived to the fullest potential of human existence, not once cowering to the shackles of fright.

For many of us, Pūjya Gurudev Swami Chinmayananda serves as a beacon, guiding us along the path. It is not that

Gurudev did not experience difficult situations, but the choices He made in those times, the choice to stay on the path and face the unknown, made Him stand apart. I do not know if I could have survived even one of the challenges that Gurudev met, and even if I had, would I have been able to do so with my faith intact and, in fact, strengthened? Yet, when I learn more about Gurudev through His writings, His talks, and, importantly, through His disciples who are here today, I am inspired and compelled to choose courage, to let go of my fears, and to keep striving forward. When we look at Gurudev's life and how He lived and approached all situations, it becomes evident, through His words and actions, that the fear itself was rendered powerless.

When we say, 'the one who has destroyed fear', what has really been destroyed is the ignorance that led to all the false notions that bind us. This ignorance of the true nature of all things, giving reality to the false objects of the world and becoming attached to the transient, is the root cause of fear. Pūjya Gurudev reminds us that it is always because of attachment that we feel fear. So, when the object of attachment that causes fear is found to be false, the fear is gone.

Through the knowledge gained from Guru, śāstras, and our sādhanas, we refocus the mind, strengthening it so that we become the masters of our own minds. We realize that fear, as with all emotions, has some purpose, and thereafter, we learn to utilize it responsibly without becoming overwhelmed by fear.

Gurudev never sought to conquer fear, as this is a battle for those of us still trudging along the plains of the mundane. For the one who has gone beyond and realized the Truth, there is no other, there is no unknown, therefore, there is no fear.

70

Om Bhāratagauravāya Namaḥ

Salutations to the one who is the pride of Bhārata.

Arvind Bhagwat

The name 'bhārata gaurava' aptly describes the mission and vision of Pūjya Gurudev, which is to glorify the great culture of Bhārat through deeds, thoughts, and legacy. In the early sixties, India was struggling to find the purpose of its newly acquired freedom. Indian saints being honored in the West was a matter of pride to most Hindus. Befittingly, Pūjya Gurudev was felicitated by various towns upon His maiden world tour. Dr. Tamboli (Bethesda, MD) recalls how the crowd felt so uplifted and enthralled at the same time upon hearing Pūjya Gurudev's humorous opening comments in one such reception in the city of Gwalior, India. Pūjya Gurudev said, "Do you think Americans don't need to pray? Every American wakes up in the morning and prays to God, 'Oh God! Please help me find a place in the parking lot!'. Material prosperity without purpose in life will never bring satisfaction or contentment. Our culture is great because it defines the purpose of human life, which is to serve God and God alone. That is the only way to become great. Feel proud of our culture, which we dedicate to God." This is indeed Bhārata gaurava.

Although I still chuckle to myself whenever I remember these words, especially while struggling to find a place in the parking lot, the real meaning of Pūjya Gurudev's words became clear during activities related to Bala Vihar in 1989-1990. The Ramakrishna Mission (RKM) Washington chapter had scheduled their two-day retreat and requested that we help them out by conducting Bala Vihar activities during their retreat. When we received this atypical request, we did not know how exactly to respond. A letter was sent to Pūjya Gurudev in India seeking permission to do such a 'favor' for RKM. Three weeks passed, and we all eagerly awaited Pūjya Gurudev's response. A day before the RKM camp began, we received Pūjya Gurudev's telegram from Melbourne, Australia, that said, "Grab the opportunity to serve the Lord!"

Now, after so many years, I can't help but read more deeply into this earnestness to serve. In my limited vision, RKM was requesting a favor. Gurudev corrected that by pointing out the principle of 'bhārata gaurava' – to bring divinity in simple acts. He was teaching us that it is an opportunity to serve and hinted that it is not 'they', but it is the Lord whom you are serving. This is the knowledge (bhā) that he wanted us to rejoice in (rata) by serving. This never struck me while engaging children during a few sessions at the RKM retreat. But now, thinking back, Pūjya Gurudev has taught us how to think! A spirit of true service uplifts our culture by guiding us to see the same Lord in all organizations and serving wholeheartedly. More importantly, He was teaching us that it is a privilege to serve the Lord, an opportunity, and one must grab it!

71

Om Bhūmne Namaḥ

Salutations to the one who is Infinite!

Swamini Seelananda

The meaning of the word bhūma is vividly explained in *Chāndogya-upaniṣad* (7.23-25). In reply to the question raised by Nārada about the nature of happiness, Bhagavān Sanatkumāra explains thus:

> *"That which is Infinite is Happiness. There is no happiness in anything finite. The Infinite alone is happiness. So, know the Infinite."*

According to Śrī Ādi Śaṅkarācārya, the word bhūma means mahat (the greatest) and niratiśayam (incomparable) denoting the transcendental Truth.

Pūjya Gurudev was a great yogī, a pramāṇa to the scriptures, and a mahāpuruṣa who came into this world to guide us. The depth and giddying heights of Gurudev's multifaceted personality remain unfathomable. With motherly concern, fatherly discipline, and masterly wisdom, He could respond to all those who came to Him according to their level of understanding and the situation in their lives.

In the morning sessions, Gurudev, pointing at the letters in the B-M-I chart, would enlighten the theme of Upaniṣads. Whenever He spoke about the supreme Reality, OM, He would turn inwards; we could observe that His yogic eyes would be half closed (in śāmbhavi mudra), indicating that He is attuned to the state of Paramātmā. He stood at the threshold of the transcendental and the relative. Once, at a casual satsaṅg during His yajña in Vijayawada in 1986, a few of us sat around Him after dinner with a few senior devotees. A lady asked Gurudev, "Swamiji, how long will it take to reach That state?" He immediately responded, "In a split second!" with half-closed eyes.

In August of 1987, there was a sādhana camp in Sidhbari. Pūjya Gurudev was explaining *Praśnopaniṣad* in the morning. While He was chanting one of the verses, a lady got up and said, "Swamiji, the verse in the text is different from how you read it." Gurudev roared, "When I sit on vyāsa-pīṭha and say something, it must be correct. You correct it in your text." That was His conviction. There was not even a little ego in His expression. He was an empty reed in the hands of the Almighty and was always established in the Supreme. The sense of 'I' in Him was nothing but the all-encompassing bhūma.

In March of 1993, during His yajña at Visakhapatnam, pāda pūjā was about to start, and the hall being full, I sat in the last row. Gurudev called me to sit in the first row close to Him. At the end of the pāda pūjā, while devotees were receiving prasād from Him, one person put a saffron silk cloth around Gurudev's shoulders. He removed the cloth, kept it with Him, and suddenly threw it at me. I caught hold of it and stared at Him. Smilingly, He said, in action, "Wear it as a sārī." I was confused because, as a brahmacāriṇi, I cannot wear saffron, but He repeated the action once again! After that day, I never had another opportunity to see Him again. But He knew it was my last time meeting Him, which is why He blessed me in such a way. After Pūjya Gurudev's mahāsamādhi, many of His devotees shared similar experiences of Him, which are significant to each one of them in their lives.

72

Om Mahāvākyopadeśakāya Namaḥ

Salutations to the teacher of the great statements of Truth.

Dr. B.K. Sathyanarayana

Mahāvākya are profound sentences or sayings that convey the essence of the teachings of Vedanta. They reveal our identity with that Divine (jīva-brahma aikya). Gurudev was the upadeśaka of Mahāvākyas, who explained the teachings enshrined therein.

The four main Mahāvākyas are:

1) Prajñānam brahma (pure Consciousness is Brahman), from *Aitareya-upaniṣad* of the Ṛg Veda, is also called lakṣaṇa (defining) vākya. That by which one sees, hears, smells, and so on is pure Consciousness, and It is Absolute.

2) Ahaṃ brahmāsmi (I am the infinite Reality!) is an anubhava (experience) vākya from *Bṛhadāraṇyaka-upaniṣad* of the Yajur Veda. "I am Brahman. I am not only a wave, I am made of ocean. I am the ocean!"

3) Ayam ātmā brahma (This Atman, the Self is Brahman!) is called anusandhāna (inquire) vākya from *Māṇḍūkya-upaniṣad* of the Atharva Veda. If Ātman is a wave, and Brahman is the ocean, the insight of 'ayam ātma brahma' is that the wave and the ocean are the same.

4) Tat tvam asi (That Brahman is you), also called upadeśa (teaching) vākya is from *Chāndogya-upaniṣad* of

the Sāma Veda. It is like telling a wave in the ocean that it is the ocean. The *Bhagavad-gītā* is the essence of 'tat tvam asi' Mahāvākya, and Gurudev taught the *Gītā* for decades.

Gurudev gave discourses and published books on the Upaniṣads and the *Bhagavad-gītā* in English, making it easy for any common man to understand our scriptures. He also gave distinctive explanations and interpretations. Gurudev was an embodiment of this spiritual wisdom. He not only taught the scriptures, but also followed it fully.

Gurudev was able to reach and touch the hearts of everyone who came into His contact through His unique way of conveying the essence of Vedānta through storytelling laced with humor. Being a journalist, He was known for His eloquent interpretations and a good command of English, which showed up greatly in His books and speeches!

When Gurudev started the Vedānta course at Sandeepany Sadhanalaya, He traveled extensively, giving discourses, to raise funds for the āśram. He would start classes the minute He returned, and the classes went on for several hours. Gurudev, noticing that the students were tired, would end the class and tell them to go and rest. But He was never tired of teaching. What a great mahāvākyopadeśaka our Gurudev was!

The Chinmaya Mission Pledge, written by Him for our upliftment, is embedded with teachings from the Upaniṣads. Gurudev's BMI chart explains, in simple terms, the basis of the Mahāvākyas – how one can detach from this world and attach to the higher Consciousness.

'You are that Brahman' is the greatest of all teachings. The one who can convey this is the greatest of all teachers. Gurudev's glorious words and actions were Mahāvākyas! And He demonstrated the glory of Mahāvākyas through His teachings! We offer our salutations unto Him!

sa etena prajñānena ātmanā asmāllokāt utkramya amuṣmin svargeloke sarvān kāmānāptvā amṛtaḥ samabhavat samabhavat

Through the Self that is Consciousness he ascended higher up from this world, and getting all desires fulfilled in that heavenly world, he becomes immortal, he becomes immortal.

~ *Aitreyopanishad* 3.1.4

73

Om Maharṣaye Namaḥ

Salutations to the one who is a great sage.

Swami Raghuveerananda

A ṛṣi is a veda mantra draṣṭā (seer or receiver of Veda mantras). Pūjya Gurudev Swami Chinmayananda, as a maharṣi, is a mantra draṣṭā, tattva draṣṭā, and a yuga draṣṭā. Let us see these three unfold through our journey as a seeker.

One evening, I stepped into a Chinmaya Mission āśram for the first time as a visitor. I heard chanting from the temple, and I felt an inexplicable attraction towards it as I drew near. I learned later that the chanting was 'Upaniṣad Ratnamāla' or 'Tapovana Śatakam', and it was so soothing, pleasant, and magnetic that I kept humming it for weeks afterward. Pūjya Gurudev Swami Chinmayananda always has you in His plans, just as He had me that day! Gurudev generates the spiritual hunger within you in ways one cannot comprehend, making you aware of your kinship with Bhagavān. Once you become conscious of it, He slowly takes you to the state where you are aware that the source of happiness and fulfillment lies inside you. The step of asserting yourself to be of the nature of Bhagavān or the Self is truly the most difficult, and Gurudev enables that as a Maharṣi.

A Maharṣi, always living in His awareness, pulls those who approach Him into that awareness. When you approach the Maharṣi, you learn the Truth and the essence of the Veda, in the words of the Veda itself. Such a Maharṣi was Gurudev! A Maharṣi can also see the future and is a true visionary, all-pervading and all-knowing. With the right vision of the Vedic Truth, Gurudev unfolds a vision for the whole world and prepares people for it. The Bala Vihars, Yuva Kendras, study groups, and the Chinmaya Vishwa Vidyapeeth all enable that dharma from the individual to the world. He is a yuga-puruṣa!

Pūjya Gurudev created an army of Vivekanandas who would carry forward the vision of the Vedas through the Sandeepany Gurukulam with a contemporary outlook. In His own words, the jñāna-yajñas were 'open-air universities' through which the seekers graduated into study groups that would further feed our immortal philosophy, and cultural riches to the army of educated people in our religion.

We can see the yuga-puruṣa, Gurudev, preparing us, irrespective of our background, into promoters of dharma through our conduct and propagation. He would prepare us in various ways so that we become competent to understand and study the śāstras. Don't we feel Gurudev's boundless compassion expressed within us?

We often doubt if it is humanly possible to completely detach from the destinies of our mind and intellect and revel in unbroken Bliss. With conviction in the Absolute Truth, Gurudev would clear such doubts in advanced seekers and sannyāsins alike. We get to see Gurudev's 'action in inaction' and 'inaction in action', His inner detachment, and unwavering perfection in every task He undertook and every institute He founded or aided. Yet His involvement is what made each one of them blossom.

Finally, even when not in physical form, we continue to experience Gurudev's loving touch that has transformed millions! Gurudev is our Maharṣi indeed!

74

Om Madhurasvabhāvāya Namaḥ

Salutations to the one who has a sweet nature.

Swami Raghavananda

The supreme Self (Paramātmā), the substratum of the whole universe, has two forms – the Absolute unmanifested Reality and the relative manifested Reality, the Lord of the entire universe. This Lord can descend anywhere, at any time, in any form. Sometimes, He embodies in human form as per the need. Those who experience oneness with the Absolute Reality are called Mahātmās (Realized Masters). Such Masters are very rare in the whole universe. Pūjya Gurudev Swami Chinmayananda was one of them.

The nature of the ultimate Truth, the supreme Self, is Sat-Cit-Ānanda. When the mind is pure, calm, quiet, concentrated, and devoid of hindrance, the Ānanda aspect of the Self is manifested as pure love in a pure heart. The sweetness of thoughts, words, and deeds can be seen in a realized person like our Gurudev.

When we utter the word sweet, our minds immediately think of some sweet dish we like. Its form, size, color, and taste also come to mind. Some people's mouths start watering just by hearing about or remembering the dish. Listening to an inert object itself has the power to stimulate our senses and mind. In the same way, remembering someone's name also influences our minds. Scriptures say the nature of Mahātmās and children are alike. Like children, they are also simple, without any hypocrisy, crookedness, likes, and dislikes. They never differentiate between caste, creed, gender, or religion. They love all and serve all.

Mahātmās like Gurudev are rare. Gurudev's love for all can be seen easily. Gurudev was like a loving, caring mother and a responsible father. As a sadguru, Gurudev guided devotees and directed disciples. Gurudev roared like a lion, striking the wrong notions and false values in the minds of devotees and disciples. In His mere presence, the minds of His devotees felt calm and elevated. Some people were attracted to and fascinated by His language, phonetic pronunciations, jokes, spiritual discourses, clear and lucid expounds, narrations, and explanations with perfect examples. His words were sweet, kind, appealing, endearing, inspiring, and sometimes fiery, roaring and hammering. He behaved like a child among children, youth among youth, and brilliant among scholars.

He was like our loving mother and father, a philosopher and a guide. All these divine qualities are due to the sweetness of His mind. It is the expression of the blissful nature of our true Self. His nature, thoughts, manners, address, words, actions, dance, pronunciations, chanting, behavior, laughter, and roar were all as sweet as Lord Śrī Kṛṣṇa.

adharam madhuram vadanam madhuram,
madhurādhipate akhilam madhuram.

By surrendering at His feet, let our hearts be filled with pure love and our minds with sweet thoughts. Let our whole life be so sweet that people around us benefit and let their life become sweet.

75

Om Manoharāya Namaḥ

Salutations to the one who has a charming persona.

Swami Atmadevananda

Manohara means the one who is captivating, steals hearts, and mighty attractive! Pūjya Gurudev is worshipped as 'the one who is enchantingly attractive'.

Long before I read this name, I had this wonderful experience in my first encounter with Him. With some devotees from Chinmaya Mission Kolhapur, I had come to Powai āśram to meet and seek the blessings of Pūjya Gurudev. He was yet to arrive. About a hundred devotees were already waiting. And then, a stream of big, expensive cars entered the gate. Gurudev emerged from one such royal car. The whole atmosphere got charged with invisible bliss. All of them flocked around Him near the vehicle. Somehow, through that crowd, I extended my hand to show Him the small copper pādukās in my palm. He put His palm on those pādukās and murmured, "Kṛṣṇa, Kṛṣṇa." He moved ahead, but I was transfixed and kept gazing at His tall figure standing out through the surrounding crowd. My eyes followed Him till He reached His kuṭiyā (room).

It was 'love at first sight'. I realized I was standing there only, but He had captured my heart. He had just given me a glance with a smile when He blessed those pādukās, but I was completely enchanted by His charm. That was the first time I realized what the term 'magnetic personality' means. Gurudev had stolen my heart!

Even before this episode, He had mesmerized me by His writings. I was staying in Kolhapur and had just come in contact with Swami Purushottamananda. At a jñāna-yajña, one of the sevaks recommended *Kindle-Life* in Marathi. Once I started reading it, I could not stop until I had completed it. I was so impressed by His inspiring logical spirituality that I immediately wrote a letter to Him, saying that I wanted to spread His literature all over. I was ready to go door-to-door to sell books. He replied promptly with blessings and advised me to work through the local Mission Center. His remark at the end of the preface of that book 'Thy Own Self' made Him my soulmate forever.

Later on, I tried to understand His secret. What I understood has become the goal of my sādhana. Generally, we are at the level of body-mind-intellect (B-M-I). When we come in contact with others, we try to extract and grab happiness through them for our B-M-I. They also want the same thing from us. In a street where all are beggars, who can give to whom? So, all are unhappy and miserable. A saint like Pūjya Gurudev realizes His Real nature as Sat-Cit-Ānanda and revels in His blissful nature. Since He is full of Bliss, He shares and spreads the nectar of love-divine, and we all are attracted towards Him as the bees are pulled towards fragrant flowers.

One should realize that happiness is within each one of us. Without expecting anything from the world, one should give love to others selflessly. People will be attracted to such a soul to seek guidance to turn to a happier spiritual life.

Gurudev wants us to become like Him, and we can achieve that only through His grace!

76

Om Mahātmane Namaḥ

Salutations to the one who is a great soul.

G.V. Raghu

What makes one a Mahātmā? The Sanskrit dictionary gives the following meanings for the word 'Mahātmā': supreme-spirit, high-souled, powerful, highly gifted, magnanimous, exceedingly wise, of noble nature, and liberal-minded.

If we look at Gurudev's life, we will know He is all these and much more!

- Supreme Spirit: Gurudev, being realized, was always reveling in that state of supreme Spirit. He was always in samādhi.
- High Souled: He was a dharma saṁsthāpaka, interested in the Hindu Renaissance, not just an expansion of the Chinmaya Mission. The Chinmaya Mission Pledge says, "We stand as one family." He always identified with all beings and saw things with an equal eye, as said in *Bhagavad-gītā* (5.18):

> *"By virtue of true knowledge, Sages see with equal vision, a learned brahmaṇa, a cow, an elephant, a dog, and an outcaste."*

- Powerful: Power comes from knowledge. He had both worldly knowledge and the Knowledge of the Self. Those who know Him have seen how He lived life with vigor, with very little rest despite His frail body in later days. His strength came from His depth of knowledge of scriptures and sciences, as shown by His voluminous literary works.

- Highly gifted: There was no subject that He was not familiar with. He instinctively knew how to deal with everyone, irrespective of the situation. His responses to situations were spontaneous and perfect. Many of His quotes were so spontaneous! When someone asked for the message of Vedānta, His answer was, "Attach and detach." When someone asked, "Swamiji, how long should I meditate?" His immediate response was, "24/7."
- Magnanimous: He was very generous in appreciating people and giving them gifts. He kept nothing to Himself and shared all that He had with others. His vision was much different from ours. He was very forgiving of the people who left Him and the Mission. He said, "What can they do with Vedānta other than spreading that knowledge and growing?"
- Exceedingly wise: His fame was not just because of His knowledge of the scriptures and way of presenting; He was extremely wise in His interactions with people. He knew how to deal with people, was extremely humble with the elderly and wise, and was very strict when teaching was needed. He always tailored His talks to the audience with an uncanny ability to completely engage them.
- Noble: Being in the state of Brahman always, His responses to situations were always noble. This is what attracted people to Him.

Many other nāmas of the Aṣṭottara, like udārahṛdaya, karuṇāsāgara, janapriya, and suhṛt, are the result of being a Mahātmā. We cannot comprehend all the qualities of such a Mahātmā. Whatever we say would be inadequate to describe Him!

77

Om Medhāvine Namaḥ

Salutations to the one who is a scholar.

Gaurang Nanavaty

A medhāvī is an intelligent person endowed with a strong memory. We admire and appreciate the razor-sharp memory and bright intellect of any such individual in the world. However, we do not generally bow down or surrender to that person. Only that intelligence or medhāśakti tuned to the Highest moves us to surrender in awe. Pūjya Gurudev Swami Chinmayananda was a medhāvī who had attuned Himself to the Source of all intelligence.

As I reflect on the nāma 'om medhāvine namaḥ', I recall how the power of Pūjya Gurudev's observation, memory, and great intelligence amazed, attracted, and transformed me and my wife Darshana to eventually surrender to the matchless medhāvī who was our Pūjya Gurudev.

It was in April 1975 that Darshana and I first attended Pūjya Gurudev's discourse in Seattle. The next evening, when we met Him, He looked at us and said, "You were there in the discourse hall last evening." To our amazement, He also indicated where we had sat and listened to Him!

Amazement soon became an inspiration as we continued to attend Pūjya Gurudev's discourses. Enchanted by the power of His intelligence rooted in the scriptures, we followed Him that weekend to Vancouver. After His discourse in Vancouver, Pūjya Gurudev asked us to join Him for the dinner bhikṣā. During that dinner, when my wife asked me how much sugar

I wanted in my tea, Gurudev noticed that and asked, "How long have you been married?" To Darshana's reply of "over three years," Pūjya Gurudev quipped: "And, you don't know how much sugar your husband takes in his tea!"

Be it in a huge crowd or at a dinner table, the alertness and quick wit of Pūjya Gurudev showed us how a Master always lived with full intelligent awareness at every moment. We started as mere listeners, but the magic of our medhāvī Gurudev motivated us to become His disciples after such early encounters since 1975. We submitted to Pūjya Gurudev and embarked on the path of spiritual living.

When a medhāvī is a spiritual Master, He wants nothing from us. He just wants us to grow spiritually. Truly expecting nothing, wanting nothing from those who surrender, the Guru tunes us to become fit spiritual instruments with the blessings that only a Guru can confer. Then, the Guru works through us.

As we look back, Darshana and I truly believe that Bhagavān sent Pūjya Gurudev – our mēdhāvī Guru, to us. As we watched, interacted, and learned at His Lotus Feet, the brilliance of His *Gītā* upadeśa and the depth of all His teachings reshaped us.

Pūjya Gurudev had the unique ability to identify how we could serve best as His disciples. He blessed Darshana with the ability to compile the Chinmaya Bala Vihar curriculum and guided me to share the knowledge of Vedānta through my satsaṅgas at Chinmaya Mission Houston since 1981.

Pūjya Gurudev's grace and medhāśakti continue to be the bliss-filled source that continues to inspire us and all His devotees to bow down in reverence. Om medhāvine namaḥ!

78

Om Yatātmane Namaḥ

Salutations to the one who is self-controlled.

Geetha Grandige

Self-restraint implies possessing a remarkable mastery over both the mind and the body, encompassing the qualities of śama (mental tranquility) and dama (physical control). Attaining this level of self-restraint requires unwavering dedication and adherence to strict self-discipline. Through consistent practice and conscious effort, one learns to govern one's thoughts and impulses, which brings harmonious alignment between the inner self and the external world. Om yatātmane namaḥ serves as a reminder of the transformative power that lies within those of us who embrace the path of self-mastery.

The ultimate objective of life is self-realization, a goal exemplified by the extraordinary journey of Gurudev. Through unwavering commitment and discipline, He profoundly understood Himself and His purpose. An inspiring example of this discipline was evident in His practice of responding to every letter He received, meticulously handwriting upwards of fifty letters each day, guiding the sādhakas in their spiritual pursuit. This same discipline and self-control empowered His emotions. Emotions, such as anger, often control the person, but when used by one with self-control, they are transformative. Once, during a jñāna yajña, a devotee in a wheelchair arrived late. Gurudev's commitment to punctuality became evident. He firmly shouted, "Get out!" making it clear that discipline and self-control are for all – no exceptions. His disapproval of tardiness was unwavering. He believed in the virtue of respecting time and schedules. People marveled at His punctuality. Attendees could set their watch by the starting and ending time of His discourses! His discipline and self-control set a powerful example for all around Him.

In the sādhaka's journey, the question may arise, "How do I achieve self-restraint?" Swami Chinmayananda taught the significance of integrating japa into daily life, teaching that it should become a natural response between thoughts or tasks. These transitional periods between thoughts and tasks present valuable opportunities to center the mind by repeating the chosen mantra. Doing so makes the mind less susceptible to distractions and fluctuations, gradually attaining a state of stillness and focus. The practice of japa acts as an anchor, bringing individuals back to their spiritual path and reminding them of their higher purpose.

Swami Chinmayananda spoke of the Olympic runner P.T.Usha to exemplify the path of Self-Realization. In her pursuit of a gold medal, Usha controlled her diet, exercised rigorously, and worked relentlessly; we too, must stay committed to self-control and discipline on our spiritual journey. Our goal of attaining Self-Realization and "to give maximum happiness to maximum people for maximum time" requires immense dedication and effort. Embracing the difficulty with determination will lead us to the fulfillment of this profound goal, transcending worldly achievements and finding lasting peace and enlightenment within ourselves and in the lives of others.

79

Om Yajñakṛte Namaḥ

Salutations to the one who has performed jñāna-yajñas.

Swami Atulananda

'Yajña' in the Vedic period was a mass communal prayer (ritual) invoking the divine powers through the fire, offering oblations into the fire, and seeking their blessings and benevolence in our lives. However, in the words of Lord Śrī Kṛṣṇa in the *Bhagavad-gītā*, the word yajña was given a new perspective, as performing every action in a 'spirit of yajña' – a self-sacrifice undertaken, along with a collective effort towards a higher goal or vision, the benefit of which must be shared with all. This principle became the very essence of karma yoga, as given to Arjuna by Lord Kṛṣṇa.

Pūjya Gurudev was a skeptic turned seeker who found answers to the meaningful questions of life in the deep study and reflections on the words of the Upaniṣads revealed to Him by His Gurus. The teachings by His Gurus and the scriptures led Him to live a life dedicated to knowledge thereafter. Inspired by the incessant flow of the mighty Ganga, He chose to bring the invaluable knowledge of the scriptures to the masses via the medium of jñāna-yajñas.

He performed many jñāna-yajñas in His forty-two years as a sannyāsin. Statistically, He has conducted over 560 *Gītā* jñāna-yajñas alone across the globe; however, this is only a recorded estimate, but those who lived with Him recall that His every breath was a teaching!

Through jñāna-yajñas, Pūjya Gurudev would create

curiosity in the listener and use it to ignite the 'fire of inquiry' in them. The inspiring words of the scriptures and the devotion in the hearts of the audience were the 'ghee and oblations' that would sustain their inquiry. Thus, He would perform the inner jñāna-yajña wherein the fire of the spiritual knowledge transmitted would burn all the 'dry woods of ignorance-based ego tendencies within'.

Through the yajña, Pūjya Gurudev awakened the hearts of all sincere seekers along with the courage and belief in themselves necessary to live an inspired life full of purpose, in utter fulfillment. Some even dared to reach the pinnacles of human existence, as shown by the scriptures, and sought enlightenment. This was the effect of the jñāna-yajñas in the hearts of millions of listeners worldwide – yajña-kṛtaḥ!

He showed the subtle difference between freedom from action and freedom in action. His words direct us to our real calling, and His love gives us faith to strive beyond our imagination even to this day. But His greatest gift to us was showing us how to eradicate our ego and seek our true Nature, which is beyond all transactions.

Getting such a teacher in our lives is a rare privilege; we must make it count. We can, we must!

"Charity must come from one's sense of abundance. True charity springs from a sense of oneness between the giver and the recipient. Unless one is able to identify oneself with others, one will not feel the noble urge to share one's possessions with others. Thus charity is born out of a capacity to restrain one's instincts of acquisition and aggrandizement, and to replace these with the spirit of sacrifice."

~ Swami Chinmayananda

80

Om Lokaprasiddhāya Namaḥ

Salutations to the one who is world renowned.

Swami Gahanananda

A Kannada poet says in his work, *Manku Thimmana Kagga*, "The lust for gold is stronger than the craving for food; stronger still is the love between man and woman. But the strongest is the craving for honor and laurels; it eats into the very vitals of the soul, Manku Thimma."

How is it that Mahātmās like Gurudev are indifferent to worldly pleasures, wealth, name, and fame that come their way unasked? The answer to this question can be found in Gurudev's reply when He was asked about the mental state of a realized person. Pūjya Gurudev said, "It is like entering a dream in full waking consciousness. You have been dreaming, but you awaken from the dream. Then you re-enter the dream state, knowing that you are the waker, the person who has awakened. What will be your attitude towards the comings and goings in the dream? In such a position, you are not compelled to do or not to do; you are just being entertained in the dream world."

Pūjya Gurudev's worldwide fame is well-known to all of us. Nancy Patchen, the author of His popular biography *Journey of a Master,* says, "The glory of Chinmaya is that He touched so many people in a personal way so that we have the courage to push ourselves beyond our mundane limitations." Mrs. Kamala, from Bengaluru, spoke for innumerable people when she said, "He was the architect of my life."

Once, as the Ācārya at Chinmaya Mission, Shimoga, Karnataka, I came across a photograph of Pūjya Gurudev in His younger days. Gurudev had signed on the photo and written the words, "Look Ahead and March!" I found the words inspiring and practical. Much of our energy is wasted in brooding over regrets of the past or in exulting over past achievements. This prevents us from living in the present. So much practical wisdom was packed into these few thought-provoking words!

In the early 1980s, Pūjya Gurudev had come to Bengaluru for His annual *Gītā* jñāna-yajña. During the week, He interacted with youngsters and encouraged them to ask questions. A young student wrote his question on a piece of paper, which was handed over to Gurudev. However, Gurudev could not answer his question due to lack of time. A few days later, he left Bengaluru for another city to do another yajña. This youngster was disappointed but soon forgot everything. However, much to his shock and surprise, he received a letter from Pūjya Gurudev more than a year later, containing a three-page answer to his question in Gurudev's flowing handwriting! The greater wonder was that the piece of paper containing the boy's question was carefully pinned to the top of the letter! Such amazing experiences show Gurudev's dedication and love for mankind, especially youngsters. This love and care earned Him a permanent place in the hearts of millions.

Pūjya Guruji Swami Tejomayananda said, "Now that Gurudev's physical presence is no longer with us, His name is doing His work to see that His Mission keeps growing all over the world. Let us all pray to Pūjya Gurudev that His grace may flow through us to the world around us.

81

Om Vāgmine Namaḥ

Salutations to the eloquent one.

Swami Prabuddhananda

Vāgmine means a good orator. In the scriptures, Bṛhaspati (Jupiter) is known by this name. In this century, for people and society at large, there was a dire need for an eloquent and impactful orator endowed with virtue, knowledge, vision, and gravity who could provide a direction for an all-around comprehensive development. This impact was explicitly evident in Gurudev's speech. As per the scriptures, a man with righteous conduct attains 'vāk-siddhi', the miraculous ability to make something happen by just saying it. Śrī Kṛṣṇa has also indicated in the *Bhagavad-gītā* (17.15),

anudvegakaram vākyam satyam priya hitam ca yat.

"Words that do not cause any excitement, are truthful, pleasant, and beneficial, along with the practice of sacred recitation, they form the austerity of speech."

- Satyam (truthfulness): One should only speak the truth. This is the first ornament of speech.
- Priyam (pleasant): The truth so spoken should be pleasing, not harsh.
- Hitam (beneficial): It should be good and beneficial for another person.

The speech should have the brevity of expression and be spoken meaningfully in the shortest possible sentences.

One should not only say the right thing at the right place, but, far more importantly, leave wrong things unsaid. Hence, the right speech is that which does not cause agitation and is truthful, pleasant, and beneficial. Those who possess all these attributes are said to have 'vāk-siddhi'. These are the embellishments with which speech should be adorned.

It is also mentioned in Patañjali's Yogasūtras that truthfulness is the prime aspect and attribute of speech, which leads to 'vāk-siddhi'. Gurudev's speech was impeccable, adorned with all four hallmarks of speech. Many who had the good fortune of listening to Him awakened and attained spiritual enlightenment.

It is clear from Vedānta that if the Guru practices penance and austerity, is devout, and is an ardent devotee, His disciple will also have the same pious instincts. The speech of such a Guru has the power to grant materialistic possessions as well.

It is the essence and impact of speech that inspired people when Swami Vivekananda said, "uttiṣṭhata jāgrata prāpya varānnibodhata" – Arise, awake! Stop not till the goal is reached.

Only the enlightened one whose speech has substance and gravity has this impact.

Pūjya Gurudev's speech was blessed by Mother Sarasvatī, the Goddess of knowledge and wisdom. He was the incarnation of Bṛhaspati.

To conclude, I would say that the word vāgmine is used for an eloquent speaker completely in command of himself, whose expressions are lucid, significant, and emphatic. Pūjya Gurudev was, by nature, a genuine master of eloquence.

82

Om Vibhave Namaḥ

Salutations to the one who is All-Pervading.

Jetindra Kumar Nayar

Vibhu means all-pervasive or omnipresent. It pervades everything inert and sentient. It pervades the gross body, subtle body, and causal body. Śrī Ādi Śankarācārya explained 'vibhum' as multiform, assuming diverse forms in all creatures, from Brahma to a motionless thing.

What pervades the entire universe is Paramātmā tattva or Brahman or Sat-Cit-Ānanda. Truly speaking, the supreme Reality, Paramātmā, and Brahman have taken all the names and forms of this universe and pervaded them as gold pervades all gold ornaments or as clay pervades all clay pots. Thus, each inert and sentient entity in this universe is the supreme Reality. By knowing this, the vision of any person will change. Pūjya Gurudev got this liberating knowledge from Param Pūjya Tapovan Maharaj, who pushed Him beyond. His vision changed, and Pūjya Gurudev identified with the total world and thus became 'vibhu'.

Someone asked, "Why are you going abroad?" and Gurudev said, "My brothers and sisters live abroad also. I want to share my knowledge with them, too." One who becomes 'vibhu' loves everyone because he sees his own 'Self' in everyone (madātmā sarvabhūtātmā). Each of Gurudev's devotees felt that Gurudev loved them the most.

While Sandeepany Sadhanalaya at Powai was being constructed, a question arose whether or not to cut a tree.

Pūjya Gurudev decided not to cut the tree but to build around it. Thus, the office building at the Powai āśram has a tree in the center, and the branches can be seen above the terrace. This is the vision of a person who is a vibhu. He knows He has become all.

Further, our Upaniṣad says, "He who knows that supreme Brahman becomes Brahman." Pūjya Gurudev was a realized soul and knower of Brahman; therefore, He was Brahman, the all-pervading. Gurudev wished that all devotees could get this vision of 'vibhu', which can be attained by expanding our vision to encompass the entire universe. He said, "Once I leave, I will be closer to all of you because I am That all-pervasive Reality only."

Bhagavān Kṛṣṇa says in the *Bhagavad-gītā* (5.18) that such a person is 'samadarśinaḥ'.

vidyā vinaya sampannē brāhmaṇē gavi hastini,
śuni caiva śvapāke ca panditāḥ samadarśinaḥ.

"With the eyes of divine knowledge, the truly learned see with equal vision a Brahmin, a cow, an elephant, a dog, and an outcaste."

Our salutations to Pūjya Gurudev who is All-Pervading!

"Formless, All-Pervading, He lives on in His teachings, through His vision, propelling further His Mission of mass elevation of human Consciousness, eons after He dropped His mortal coil, He remains never forgotten and ever felt!"
~ Source: Chinmaya Ashtottara Namavali, Chinmaya YouTube Channel

83

Om Vinodapriyāya Namaḥ

Salutations to the one who loves humor.

Kuntimaddi Sadananda

The word vinoda has many meanings. Some meanings mentioned in the Śiva Purāṇa are fun, joy, recreation, sport or play, happiness, or singing out jubilantly.

The word can also be split as vi-noda, which means driving away (obstacles) and removing sorrow (in others).

All the above meanings are relevant to Gurudev.

It was always fun to be around Gurudev. People used to sit around Him for hours since every minute was joyful. After finishing His work, Gurudev would come out of the room since He knew that people were waiting for Him. He would stay there until it was time to do more work, mostly responding to letters to remove the suffering of others – for vi-noda.

Before He took sannyāsa, Gurudev used to play tennis and was very good at it. Hence, He loved to watch the Wimbledon Tennis tournaments. After He completed His discourses, Gurudev would watch tennis for relaxation or vinoda. Disciples would pre-record the tournaments so that Gurudev could watch leisurely whenever He wanted or was free.

He would tell us that life is vinoda or sport; like any sport, one must play their best at any time. The stronger the opponent, the better should be one's play. The extent of the programs that He initiated around the world was phenomenal. He was on top of each program to ensure that the work initiated was being done with utmost care. That is vinoda; hence, the name rightly says – vinodapriyāya namaḥ.

He said, "A spiritual seeker should not try to run away in the very beginning into protection but must court life and plunge into the center of it and take life as it comes...good, bad, or indifferent, and learn to balance himself despite all imperfections in the circumstances. Only then does life become a vinoda (sport)."

It was fun to watch Him interact and play with children. He became a child around children. For those who are witnessing these interactions, that in itself is a vinoda. He would say, "Life is a sport, and one should enjoy every minute. Winning is not the measure of success, but playing one's best is – in the process, one becomes a better and better player, ready to deal with whatever comes in the way." That is the essence of being 'vinodapriya' – the one who enjoyed life as a real sport and, in the process, relieved the suffering of others – vinodapriya – to Him, my salutations!

Devotee: From where does laughter spring?
Gurudev: "If thoughts and agitations of the mind all of a sudden get dumbfounded, for instance at an unexpected joke or something, the mind becomes suddenly quiet for just that split second. This sudden arrest of thoughts is like shock therapy to the mind, which releases psychic energy that expresses itself as laughter, horripilation, dance, or music."

84

Om Vinayaśīlāya Namaḥ

Salutations to the one who is humble.

Brahmacharini Pranati Chaitanya

Humility is a quality that manifests in every truthful person. It is impossible to be humble without being truthful. Without recognizing and holding onto the truth, every human becomes a victim of pride. Humility means accepting the truth. When a person acknowledges, remembers, and pays gratitude to the people who have been instrumental in helping him achieve his goals, he is considered humble. Such a person never declares himself humble; his behavior and mannerisms reflect this quality.

Gurudev was the epitome of humility. He was humility personified. This aspect was evident whenever Gurudev met saints. Although He was a realized saint, when He visited Bhagavān Ramana Maharshi and Anandamayi Mā, He would sit at their feet and listen to their discourses. Once, Gurudev invited Pūjya Swami Gangeshwarananda to Sandeepany Sadhanalaya to preach to the students. The students placed two similar sofas, one each for Pūjya Gurudev and Swami Gangeshwarananda. After escorting Pūjya Swami Gangeshwarananda to his āsanā, Gurudev sat at the feet of Swami Gangeshwarananda instead of the āsanā that was assigned to Him. Gurudev is considered one of the most revered and respected saints of the modern era. He roared like a lion while preaching the principles of the scriptures. He had a hold over the knowledge of the scriptures and was a living embodiment of them. Despite that, when He met other saints, He listened to them with utmost keenness.

Gurudev used to invite great saints to Sandeepany Sadhanalaya and requested them to preach to the students of the Gurukul. He always encouraged His disciples to visit and listen to the teachings and experiences of other great saints.

Innumerable episodes depict the humility of Pūjya Gurudev. When Gurudev used to conduct spiritual camps in Sidhbari, a ritual of pāda pūjā was observed instead of pāduka pūjā. On one such occasion, when Gurudev was being escorted by Chinmaya Yuva Kendra (CHYK) students for pāda pūjā, a devotee was standing on the path from where Gurudev had to pass to reach the satsaṅg hall. He was deeply absorbed in watching the majestic beauty of the snow-capped peaks of the Himalayas. A fine, gentle, and fragrant breeze filled the atmosphere. The devotee went into a meditative mood and failed to see that Gurudev was coming that way. This prompted the CHYK students to rush towards him, asking him to leave the passage immediately. The devotee felt sorry and moved away from the path. When Gurudev noticed this, he went and apologized to the devotee and said, "Because of me, you lost your state and had to come out of your meditative mood." He was a saint of such high stature who could apologize to anyone. This is a great example of Gurudev's humility!

These incidents give us an insight into Pūjya Gurudev's personality and character, revealing His attribute of humility!

yato vāco nivartante, aprāpya manasā saha,
ānandaṁ brahmaṇo vidvān na bibheti kutaścaneti.

He who knows the Bliss of Brahman, from which all words return without reaching It, together with the mind, is no more afraid of anything.

~ *Taittiriyopanishad* 2.9.1

85

Om Vītarāgāya Namaḥ

Salutations to the one who is free from all attachments.

Mahadevan Parameswaran

Pūjya Gurudev would say, "Attach and detach." It is the very essence of Vedānta. Attach to the eternal Bliss that is your nature by constantly abiding in It, and detach from the identification with the body-mind-intellect (BMI).

Sādhana Panchakam says, "escaping from the bondage of 'home' (the BMI), one seeks the Self with consistent endeavor." Śrī Kṛṣṇa talks about this in the *Bhagavad-gītā* (2.56), in the stithaprajña lakṣaṇa (the indicator marks of a realized soul): one who is free of attachment, fear, and anger is a sage of steady wisdom, a stithaprajña, a jīvanmukta.

One could see Gurudev's detachment from many incidents in His life. Once, I was fortunate to visit Him at a camp in Houston, where I saw and felt His detachment. Due to the poor condition of His physical heart, Gurudev was constantly getting reports about His heart health through His caretaker at each camp. A report had just come in, and Jyoti, who was taking care of Gurudev, read out the report, saying, "Swamiji, I have good news. There is no fluid in the lungs." Gurudev said, "In the past, many sages left their bodies, setting fire to them; here I am dying in my own juice." He was totally calm as He uttered those words, a clear sign of a 'vītarāga puruṣa', the one who is detached from the body.

A devotee at a satsaṅg, unconvinced about God's presence, asked Pūjya Gurudev, "Swamiji, show me a miracle!" Gurudev replied, "See, all these floating pieces of flesh, you and me, and all others, are enlivened and activated to perform miracles by Śrī Nārāyaṇa, who pervades everything." This shows perfect detachment of the flesh from the spirit.

Pūjya Gurudev always referred to our relation to the Supreme as "The relation-less relationship," much like the ocean and the waves, where the waves cannot exist apart from the oceanic water. Still, the water does not need the waves to exist, like the Self, totally detached from the BMI.

Pūjya Gurudev diligently recorded the fifty-four *Bhagavad-gītā* video tapes at our Piercy Retreat Center in California. He came out occasionally for a breather between talks, dismissing it as normal tiredness. But the doctors attending to Him said He was having minor heart attacks. He had to finish what He started!

When I was the coordinator of the Bala Vihar program, Gurudev came to me and said, "That's enough now; let someone else handle it." My reactive mind said, "Why am I being taken away from doing something Gurudev was happy about?" After analyzing and talking to people, I realized that He was teaching me the art of detaching from something that I liked to do. He was trying to get me to play the role of a leader, to guide someone else in performing that task.

So, how can one describe such a great soul who can detach and attach at His own will? A Samskṛta subhāṣitam says:

"The minds of extraordinary persons are stronger than a diamond and more tender than a flower. Who may be able to understand them?"

86

Om Vedāntavedyāya Namaḥ

Salutations to the one who is known through Vedānta.

Medha Bhagwat

Vedānta means 'the essence of Vedas'. The Sanskrit word 'Veda' comes from the root 'vid', which means 'to know'. Veda also means the treasure of knowledge. Vedas contain the knowledge of all aspects of worldly and spiritual life, what one needs to know and wants to achieve, and also provide a means to achieve it.

There are three portions (kāṇḍas) of the Vedas: karma kāṇḍa, upāsana kāṇḍa and jñāna kāṇḍa. The jñāna kāṇḍa portion of the Vedas, also called Upaniṣad or Vedānta, answers fundamental questions of life, such as 'Who am I?' and 'What is the purpose of life?'. Thus, Vedānta reveals the ultimate Truth or nature of our Self. The Self can be known through the Vedas but not through any other means of knowledge. Thus, Om vēdāntavedyāya namaḥ means salutations to that Self, which is known through (the study of) Vedānta.

Vedānta declares I am infinite and ever blissful. Then why don't we experience it or realize it? Our likes and dislikes make our minds impure and cover the knowledge of our Self. Due to ignorance of our infinite and ever-blissful nature, we consider ourselves finite and experience sorrow. We then try to complete ourselves by getting attached to the outside world through our body, place, objects, circumstances, and other people. We apply various means and actions to achieve that (aprāptasya prāpti). Through these interactions, we try to make ourselves happy and wait for happiness in the future. But we never seem to reach it. The outside world is constantly changing. We don't realize that several outside temporary objects cannot give us permanent happiness.

Only through the study of Vedānta under the guidance of a Guru can we realize that happiness lies within; it is my own nature (prāptasya prāpti). However, according to our scriptures, a Guru who can reveal this highest knowledge to a disciple must have these two qualifications: he must be well-versed in the scriptures (śrotriya) and firmly established in the knowledge of the Truth (brahmaniṣtha).

Swami Chinmayananda was not only a Realized Master but also brought knowledge of our scriptures in English from the Himalayas to the common person. He set up avenues to study Vedānta. Sandeepany Sadhanalaya was set up for a deeper understanding of Vedānta and to train future teachers. He traveled tirelessly across the globe conducting various jñāna-yajñas despite being in poor health. He envisioned programs for various stages and aspects of life – Bala Vihar, Chinmaya Vidyalaya, Chinmaya University, Chinmaya Yuva Kendra, Chinmaya Vanaprastha, and Chinmaya International Foundation. There are now several Chinmaya Mission centers across the globe spreading the knowledge of Vedānta. He worked tirelessly so that all of us could reach there. He told us, "Don't put the key to your happiness in someone else's pocket." Through the study of Vedānta, we realize that happiness isn't something we seek externally; we are That Happiness. This will lead to the ultimate peace.

87

Om Śāntāya Namaḥ

Salutations to the one who is peace.

Swami Suveerananda

I have heard of an incident from Pūjya Gurudev's life from one of our senior Swāmins. One day, Pūjya Gurudev was in his kuṭiyā at Sandeepany Sadhanalaya. He was writing something. At that time, a devotee entered the room to talk to Gurudev. While leaving the room, he turned back and asked Gurudev, "Did I disturb you?" Gurudev looked at that person and said, "You did, but I am not disturbed." This gives us a glimpse into the greatest virtue Pūjya Gurudev possessed, which was always being peaceful.

When we talk about being peaceful, it looks like an unknown term for most of us in the modern day because we lose calmness at the drop of a hat. In the second chapter of the *Bhagavad-gītā*, the Lord beautifully presents this quality in the sthitaprajña lakṣaṇa, where He says, "He alone, who with perfect self-control goes through life among the infinite number of sense objects, each impinging upon him and trying to bind him with its charm, and approaches them with neither love nor hatred, comes to enjoy peace." (*Bhagavad-gītā* 2.64).

He also says, "It is a very well-known example that although millions of gallons of river water flow into the ocean every day, the water level in the ocean does not change. Similarly, even though an infinite number of sense objects may pour in their stimuli through the five sense channels, they undoubtedly reach the mental zone of the perfect man, but they do not create commotion or flux in his bosom. This is because he is full, and there is no craving for anything from the world outside." (*Bhagavad-gītā* 2.70).

Pūjya Gurudev embodied these qualities; He remained calm, peaceful, and, deep down, quiet. Gurudev was ever peaceful even during the greatest of losses. He remained calm whether people admired Him, talked badly of Him, or even when they betrayed Him. Calmness was His very nature.

Being the devotees of Pūjya Gurudev, the apt way to surrender unto Him is through our steadfast sādhana to embody this virtue – to keep our minds calm at all places and times and not get agitated. And that is something worth achieving!

Gurudev's response to Anjali Singh's question on meditation:
"To achieve the state of Conscious being, the physical, mental, intellectual and spiritual personalities of a person must all be blended into one harmonious whole. Meditation is the technique of achieving this harmony. It is the highest spiritual discipline. Through meditation a person comes to experience peace within and without."

88

Om Śāntipradāya Namaḥ

Salutations to the one who gives peace to all.

Priya Kumar Maini

True peace and quietude can come from knowledge alone. The epitome of this silence, Pūjya Gurudev's every breath was dedicated to bestowing this silence to others through the Knowledge of Vedānta.

The journey of a seeker begins with a multitude of questions and an honest hope to find answers to each and every one of them! I, too, began my serious study of Vedānta with a bag full of questions. As the Vedānta course progressed, the questions faded like a distant memory. The powerful, transformational teachings had shattered all of my illusions and misconceptions about the world. I was completely convinced that there was not a single challenge or question that didn't have a spiritual solution. There were no more doubts, no wavering, nothing left to say.

In our ancient tradition, the chanting of a śānti mantra is prescribed before beginning any task. The invocation of peace removes all obstacles and silences the mind, thus creating the perfect environment for the flower of knowledge to bloom. All obstacles originate from three sources: ādhidaivika – divine and unseen forces of nature, such as earthquakes, volcanoes, and floods over which we have little control; ādhibhautika – known factors such as crime, pollution, and the people around us; and ādhyātmika – immediate problems pertaining to our bodies and minds such as disease, anger, and agitation. By the Lord's grace and the Guru's blessings, these obstacles can be removed or decreased, at least during the time of study.

The peace invocation attunes the Guru and seeker to one another, such that the seeker naturally imbibes the peace emanating from the Guru, and the Guru understands how best to impart spiritual knowledge to this particular seeker. A Guru's teachings, love, and constant blessings lay the foundation for the seeker's dawn of enlightenment. Pūjya Gurudev roared Vedānta, casting a deafening silence in the heart of every student.

I have not met Pūjya Gurudev in person, but I have known Him through His teachings. Pūjya Gurudev is so captivating that all my distractions fall away, and my focus immediately converges upon His speech and writings. As a child who felt lost everywhere else, in Bala Vihar I was found. As a youth seeking permanent happiness in the ephemeral mists of money and power, in Chinmaya Yuva Kendra, I was grounded. As a student of Vedānta, drowning in the noise of my own thoughts, doubts, and oscillations, I was bestowed the gift of silence.

> *"Remove all anxiety. The burdens of samsāra*
> *are all of our own subjective making.*
> *The disturbed mind has no power and feels helpless.*
> *When it surrenders to the Lord, it becomes quiet."*
> *~ Swami Chinmayananda*

89

Om Śāstroddhārakāya Namaḥ

Salutations to the one who uplifts the scriptures.

Swami Vijayananda

All the scriptures available now in this world are derived from the ancient scriptures called Vedas. Ananto vai vedāḥ – veda śāstras are vast and countless. But among them, only a few are available today. Time and again, many great visionary seers have been born to reinterpret the essence of the śāstras to the new generations to apply the injunctions of the śāstras in their daily lives. When a śāstra is not applicable in our day-to-day life, it cannot be called a śāstra. So, it is the Master who puts effort into reinterpreting them in a timely manner for the coming generations for their practice.

Once upon a time, all our Hindu śāstras were confined to only a few communities, and they thought it was their job to protect it by memorizing the Vedas embedded in script form. Centuries passed without knowing what was in the śāstras. Those scholars put their efforts only by memorizing them instead of putting them into practice, which continued for generations. Not even a single ray of scriptures beamed in the lives of mankind. They did not try to find out what was in it.

On the other hand, they were not made accessible to others. Only after the efforts of the great visionary Śrī Ādi Śankarācārya did they become available to all other communities. He spread this Vedik knowledge in all directions of our country through his disciples. Likewise, later, many Mahātmās spread this unique knowledge in their era.

In the nineteenth century, one visionary Seer, Pūjya Gurudev, Swami Chinmayananda, added modernity to the scriptures and made that knowledge accessible to all in an innovative way. Pūjya Gurudev, having studied and understood the aim and goal of śāstras, brought down that jñāna Ganga to the plains of the world and taught the superiority of human life as stated in the śāstras. He guided people to practice the message of the śāstras in their day-to-day lives. It was the vision of Pūjya Gurudev that every human being should read the scriptures and practice the virtues mentioned in them, thus making their life meaningful. Pūjya Gurudev never encouraged anyone to have a blind belief in the śāstras.

On the other hand, He asked us to listen, contemplate and realize. Then alone, śāstroddhāraṇa is possible. Unless we practice the valuable injunctions of the śāstras, they only remain like showpieces in our library. Śāstras are meant for a dynamic way of living, which can be fulfilled only in our Hindu way of Life.

"My attempt is to build a study and research center to bring out the relevance of the ancient terms of our Sanskrit literature in the context of the modern way of life. The Chinmaya International Foundation has been set up to bridge the fully-developed, time-tested, trusted, ancient science of the East and the modern developing branches of science in the West – a bridge between East and West, past and present, science and spirituality, pundit and public."

~ Swami Chinmayananda

90

Om Śuddhasattvāya Namaḥ

Salutations to the immaculate (pure) one.

Rahul Maini

A mind that possesses a dull disposition is tāmasika. A rājasika mind energetically works to fulfill worldly desires. A sāttvika mind thirsts for knowledge and has achieved relative peace through devoted service to the Guru and the Lord.

Beyond these three mental temperaments is śuddhasattva or viśuddhasattva, in which one has transcended even the sāttvika desire for knowledge. Thus, one has become utterly desireless, and without the fuel of desire, the mind ceases to think. A mind without thoughts is no longer a mind; therefore, śuddhasattva cannot be considered a mental temperament. That state of śuddhasattva in which the agitation of thoughts is absent is the very state of Absolute Peace.

Furthermore, each of the guṇas holds a particular power or śakti. Tamoguṇa is possessed with āvaraṇa-śakti, which veils an individual from knowing that he is the Infinite Self. The vikṣepa śakti of rajoguṇa projects a false and limited identity for the veiled Self. Sattvaguṇa is the source of viveka śakti, by which an individual intellectually distinguishes between the false identity and the True Self.

When the stormy projections driven by vikṣepa have been completely quieted, then the mighty power of discrimination (viveka-śakti) pierces through the veil of ignorance brought about by the āvaraṇa-śakti. The viveka-śakti, having fulfilled its purpose, does not linger; instead, it subsides, giving way to Bliss alone. Thus, the state of śuddhasattva transcends the three śaktis.

Just like the sun's reflection is seen in a pool of water, when the Self reflects upon the mind, there is the phenomenon of reflected Consciousness. When the sun shines on muddy waters, the reflected sun appears dirty, and when the sun shines on turbulent waters, the reflected sun appears to be disturbed. Similarly, when the mind is sullied by tamas and disturbed by rajas, the reflected Consciousness also appears to be obscured and disturbed, and the individual takes himself to be afflicted and miserable.

When the dirt is completely filtered out, and the water becomes absolutely still, the sun's reflection is totally clear. Similarly, as the individual grows through selfless service and sincere and continuous contemplation on the scriptures, the rajas and tamas shrink while the sāttvika aspect flourishes. Such a highly sāttvika mind is not the final goal but the last milestone to cross. When only sattva remains in the mind, then the reflection of Consciousness becomes so clear that the finite mind dissolves in its attempt to grasp the infinite Self. Upon the mind's dissolution, even the sattva disappears, and in this state of śuddhasattva, the Self alone remains.

Pūjya Gurudev attained the state of śuddhasattva – desirelessness characterized by going beyond tamas, rajas, and even sattva. With śuddhasattva as the foundation, Gurudev made perfect decisions and crafted perfect visions. Decades before its establishment, Gurudev proclaimed the need for a profound and grand institution – Chinmaya Vishwa Vidyapeeth – that keeps Vedānta as the foundation for all other knowledge. Such a vision emanating from the Immaculate ensures that materialistic achievements are guided by spiritual truths for the long-term benefit of society.

91

Om Śrutipāragāya Namaḥ

Salutations to the one who spreads the teachings of the scriptures.

Brahmacharini Maitreyi Chaitanya

"Hold on to the scriptures, and they will take you higher," advised Pūjya Gurudev.

Śruti, Smṛti, Itihāsa, and Purāṇa are the four cornerstones of our knowledge systems. Amongst these, the Śruti is supreme and holds the principal source of knowledge.

Pāraga means the one who has gone beyond. What does it mean to go beyond the Śruti?

Śruti is mainly divided into three parts – karma kāṇḍa, upāsana kāṇḍa, and jñāna kāṇḍa. As explained by Pūjya Guruji Swami Tejomayananda, these three parts of the Śruti are for us to get rid of our three 'manufacturing defects', namely mala (likes and dislikes), vikṣēpa (agitations) and āvaraṇa (ignorance). Pūjya Gurudev was beyond all three parts of the Śruti and had destroyed all three defects.

Pūjya Gurudev reached the epitome of karma kāṇḍa by giving up all likes and dislikes. Not just the personal likes and dislikes about food or clothing, but even when it was pertaining to the work of the Mission, it was done with total impartiality.

We are aware of Gurudev's Śiva upāsana in His childhood. The culmination of this upāsana was that whoever met Him, even for a few moments, would feel free from all agitations.

Jñāna kāṇḍa refers to the knowledge of Brahman as stated in the Upaniṣads. However vast the Upaniṣad may be, all the literature indicates one meaning – 'I am Brahman'. Thus, to go beyond jñāna kāṇḍa is to go beyond the word meanings, understand the stated meaning, and abide in the same. Pūjya Gurudev's life is an exemplary life of abiding in the Supreme.

Though people saw Him acting, working, initiating, creating, and carrying out the numerous tasks in the world outside, He was never tainted by it. Inside, He was as calm and deep as the ocean. He is indeed the very antaryāmi (the inner witness) of us all. He would say, "I am in the world but not of the world."

The greatness of saints is found in their selfless efforts to make others great. Just like Pūjya Gurudev's famous example of pole vault, one can go beyond scriptures only by holding onto them for a sufficient amount of time.

Hence, Gurudev made us all hold the scriptures and fall back on them whenever required. He is a rare Master who made all His disciples and followers hold on to the divine scriptures and not be merely person-oriented.

He taught us to respect, love, understand, and, most importantly, live the scriptures! Only a Master who has thoroughly gone through and beyond the scriptures can make this happen.

92

Om Śrotriyāya Namaḥ

Salutations to the one who knows and has studied the Vedas.

Sharada Kumar

Śrotrīyam (well-versed in Vedas) always goes with brahmaniṣṭha, the one who is firmly established in Brahman, the Absolute.

In *Muṇḍaka-Upaniṣad*, mantra (1.2.12), says:

tad vijñānārthaṁ sa gurum evābhigacchet,
samitpāṇiḥ śrotriyam brahma-niṣṭham

"To gain the knowledge of the Self, one must humbly approach, with sacrificial grass (samit) in his hands, a spiritual master who is well versed in the Vedas and is established in Brahman."

The word 'eva' is beautifully placed between 'Gurum' and 'abhigacchet' so it can go with either or both words. Also, 'eva' means 'only' and can also mean 'it must be done'. So, 'abhigacchet eva' means one must go, and 'Gurum eva' means only to the Guru to realize Brahman. Therefore, one must approach only a Guru to realize Brahman.

The following line expounds the nature of the Guru as śrotrīyam and brahmaniṣṭham. If he is just brahmaniṣṭha, it is great for him! But how does it help others if he cannot communicate with them? So, śrotriyam is very important. He must be well-versed in the scriptures and be able to convey the scriptural messages to others who approach him to gain this knowledge.

With Gurudev, the scriptures came alive. The points that He made were etched so deeply that even after thirty years, they remain fresh in our memories. A personal example of this was during the *Vivekacūḍāmaṇi* marathon camp in Sidhbari in 1992. During that camp, as I was chanting verse thirty-six – "durvāra saṃsāradavāgni tāptam" (save me from death, afflicted as I am by the unquenchable fire of this world-forest) – in whatever melody I managed to fit it in, Gurudev stopped me abruptly. He roared, "Show that urgency! You are burning! Your sārī is on fire!" He teased with a dragging rendition of "durvaa-aara-samsaa-aara..." and then showed me how to sing it as if I were actually on fire. A lesson right in the moment – He wanted us to feel that we were being licked by the flames of the fire of samsāra! The scriptures were not just written in the books for Him but were living words that danced in front of Him!

While describing Mother Sarasvatī, the Goddess of learning and knowledge, Pūjya Gurudev Himself wrote, "Śrotriyam (one who knows the philosophy of the Upaniṣads well) and brahmaniṣṭham (one who is well-established in the subjective experience of the Self) are the two qualities of a true teacher. In short, She represents not merely a person of Realization in samādhi but a true Guru who plays their knowledge upon the heartstrings of the disciples. She gathers the instrument, tunes up its strings, and starts singing. Soon, the wafting music enchants others to approach Her feet to learn this music and produce the same celestial melody."

Thus, our śrotriya Gurudev has defined śrotriyam!

93

Om Sannyāsine Namaḥ

Salutations to the one who is a renunciate.

Shashi Duraiswami

The word sannyāsin means the one who has completely given it all up! Swami Chinmayananda was that sannyāsin of the modern twentieth century who, having given it all up, worked tirelessly till His last breath to spread the Knowledge of Vedānta. Gurudev's revolutionary vision ensured that scriptures of the Vedas were available to all seekers worldwide regardless of national origin, caste, creed, or gender. From His first jñāna-yajña titled "Let us be Hindus," to one of His last *Vivekacūḍāmaṇi* discourses, He not only inspired the younger generation and the youth towards spirituality but also showed the gṛhastha (householders) how to pave their way to liberation.

Gurudev emphasized the importance of studying scriptures and performing our duties to purify our minds. He also provided us the opportunity get involved in the service of humanity by spreading the knowledge of the Vedas.

Gurudev established Sandeepany Sadhanalaya, a gurukula-type setting, open to all seekers. Today, His vision not only guides young seekers to become brahmacārins and sannyāsins but also householders like me, to work on their spiritual goals. By providing the very same opportunities, we too, can confidently move from gṛhastha to vānaprastha to sannyāsa āśrama.

As taught by Śrī Kṛṣṇa in the *Gītā*, renouncing does not

imply running away from our duties. With His witty and powerful discourses, Gurudev showed all gṛhasthas how to convert their actions into yajñas with a karma yoga attitude. Dedicating all our actions to the Lord and renouncing all expectations of the results thereof, helps us live our lives fully, freely, and blissfully while progressing in our spiritual path.

In today's world of emphasis on active lifestyles, there are plenty of options to keep ourselves busy and occupied. But in the long run, they are neither healthy, meaningful, nor satisfying. We often see people in their old age struggling to come to terms with their deteriorating situation when they are unable to keep up with their so-called 'active lifestyle'.

If we sow the seed of spirituality in gṛhastha āśrama, as shown by Gurudev, then as our responsibilities decrease, we can transition to vānaprastha by enhancing our spiritual sādhana. Reflecting on our scriptures and concentrating our mind on upāsana of the Lord, we train ourselves not to depend on worldly objects and relationships. We experience bliss as we continue to purify and concentrate our minds.

Our duties will recede as we age and progress, causing us to enter sannyāsa āśrama. Continued nididhyāsana (meditation) to abide in the knowledge gained in gṛhastha, with reflection and focused mind gained in vānaprastha, we will be poised to enjoy our sannyāsa also in bliss, regardless of our physical or environmental situation. "He should be known as a perpetual sannyāsī who neither hates nor desires, for, free from the pair of opposites, O mighty-armed, he is easily set free from bondage." (*Bhagavad-gītā* 5.3)

The path from karma to karma-yoga to karma sannyāsa to karma sannyāsi, as taught by Lord Kṛṣṇa to Arjuna, Gurudev revealed that path to me. To that sannyāsī, I offer my salutations.

94

Om Samabuddhaye Namaḥ

Salutations to the equanimous one.

Shashikala Dwarakanath

Pūjya Gurudev's equanimity of mind was legendary. It could be seen in all situations and at all times. Not only that, we could even feel it in ourselves while in His presence.

Ordinary people like us do have, on occasion, some moments of equanimity, but it is fleeting, easily broken, dependent, and inconsistent. However, equanimity is the nature of the person who is established in Truth and understands the presence of the same Truth in all and everything around. This is the hallmark of a person of Realization. Bhagavān Śrī Kṛṣṇa in the *Bhagavad-gītā* extols this virtue starting from the second chapter. In the sixth chapter of the *Gītā*, verses seven through nine highlight the physical, mental, and intellectual equipoise of such a person under all circumstances, their ability to understand the place of all objects and their utility, and equal vision as they interact with people of differing attitudes and aptitudes.

In 1992, we had the blessed opportunity of hosting Pūjya Gurudev at our home. After a hectic three-day stay when Gurudev left, I suddenly became aware of the state of my own mind. I had felt a sense of calm and peace throughout, despite many strangers staying at our home and many people visiting Swamiji at all times. How could that be, and how can I maintain that? As I pondered this aloud, a devotee said, "This is how we feel in His presence." His still mind transmits peace to all around! How powerful is this state of equanimity of the one who is established in his true Self!

As a physician, knowing that His heart was functioning at only a fraction of its normal capacity, it was a miracle seeing Pūjya Gurudev at His desk in the early morning hours, His constant interaction with guests and devotees, and delivering thunderous talks at Universities. Who else but the one who is established in their True Self could ignore the body's limitations, focus energy on the essentials, maintain a sense of humor, and bring the most uplifting message for humanity under all circumstances? Equanimity is a natural expression of such a person.

The most important revelation of the expression of His equanimous state continues to unfold to this day for me. A Realized Master, out of compassion and love, accepts one and all and meets them where they are on their spiritual path. As Mimi Robins, a long-time devotee of Gurudev, would say, "Swamiji did a unique dance with each devotee." This has enabled me to hold on to and surrender to Him through the years. It has opened up many doors and, to this day, leads and guides me forward in my spiritual journey.

Finally, as a sādhaka, I am constantly reminded, "siddhasya lakṣaṇāni sādhakasya sādhanāni" – the attributes of Realized Masters are practices to be brought into the lives of seekers.

> *"...To recognize yourself with the One, with the whole universe, feeling that I will not harm anyone, and I am in harmony with the entire universe is the highest state. Living then becomes effortless and creative. When one goes beyond the action-reaction stage, beyond good and evil, and cause and effect, then life becomes a recreation and a means of expressing the inner joy."*
> *~ Swami Chinmayananda*

95

Om Saccidānandāya Namaḥ

Salutations to the one who is Pure Existence, Consciousness, and Bliss.

Siva Velu

Gurudev is working through hundreds and thousands of hands all over the world, even today. Every sevak from any Chinmaya Mission Center in any part of the world feels His presence in whatever sevā they undertake. At any point in time, somewhere in the world, the Chinmaya Mission activities in the form of jñāna-yajña, satsaṅg, study groups, Bala Vihar, youth programs, and so on are going on with Gurudev's blessings. Whether in snowy Calgary or hot Chennai, Gurudev is always present in everything we do. Can we ever experience His absence or non-existence? It is impossible because He is the eternal Infinite Existence (sat).

When we as sevaks take up a project, it doesn't matter what size it is; we do our best, and when we face some obstacle, we will say, "Gurudev will take care of the rest!" Sure enough, Gurudev will continue to illuminate our path and help us achieve our goals. Time and again, we see resources appearing from unknown and unexpected corners. Gurudev enlivens every task we do to implement His vision. He is Existence-Consciousness (sat-cit) in everything we do.

Whenever we encounter any devotee from any part of the world who was fortunate to have darśan of Gurudev while living, the devotee always has something unique, inspiring, and blissful to share. As the devotee narrates their experience from several decades ago, we can feel the joy they are tapping from that formless infinite source of Bliss. That source of Bliss was Gurudev, and He radiated happiness. Many of us were not blessed to meet Gurudev in person, and yet, we derive joy and peace when we live by His teachings, when we are doing our sevā, or when we listen to Gurudev. Even though Gurudev is not with us, He continues to radiate the same Ānanda to everybody (Sat-Cit-Ānanda).

Someone once asked Gurudev how He managed to travel so much. Gurudev's reply was, "I don't travel. I don't go anywhere." Another time, when asked, "Swamiji, how is your health?" Gurudev replied, "I am using this (body) as much as I can." These interactions and the fact that Gurudev was continuously in bliss despite His painful ill health during His later years reveal that He was always abiding in the Truth.

While living in form, Swami Chinmayananda revealed to us the formless Infinite Self, the eternal Existence-Consciousness-Bliss. Gurudev taught us that even in the midst of activities, we can falsify our ego and go beyond the conditionings of the body to realize our True Self, which is of the nature of Sat-Cit-Ānanda.

> *"Leap from the shores of duality into the rigged boat of discrimination and ply ceaselessly towards the horizon of experience. Let the helmsman be śraddhā and keep the boat steady towards the Pole Star, the mahāvākya. Carefully navigate around the dangerous rocks of your own lower nature. You shall reach the Eternal Haven of Peace and Bliss: Truth."*
> *~ Swami Chinmayananda*

96

Om Sarvahitacintakāya Namaḥ

Salutations to the one who thinks of the welfare of all.

Sukanya Sathya

Gurudev, as a vedāntin, was well established in the Self. Lovingly, He wanted to help others understand their true nature. This shows His sarvātmabhāva – seeing oneness in all. He demonstrated how to dispel selfishness and set an example to the world through an immaculate life of service. He embodied this great quality, which we should strive to develop.

Gurudev preached continuously for forty-four years, giving the greatest dāna (offering), jñāna dāna. He made our sacred texts accessible to all by teaching the *Bhagavad-gītā* and Upaniṣads in English. For Him, the whole world is His family – vasudhaiva kuṭumbakam.

Vivekacūḍāmaṇi (37) says, "There are good souls, calm and magnanimous, who do good to others as does the spring, and who, having themselves crossed this dreadful ocean of birth and death, help others also to cross the same, without any motive whatsoever." This perfectly describes Gurudev.

Pūjya Gurudev, as a great visionary, successfully established many groups to help people grow spiritually. Considering the welfare of future generations, He started (1) Bala Vihar, weekly classes for children, and the Chinmaya Vidyalaya schools, which show us the value He placed on children's spiritual growth. (2) Chinmaya Yuva Kendra, an organization to empower the youth. (3) Chinmaya study groups for adults to read, discuss, and understand our scriptures. (4) CORD (Chinmaya Organization for Rural Development) to help rural communities uplift themselves. (5) Devi group for women to take up regular spiritual study and social work.

When some female devotees expressed concern about not having time for their spiritual sādhana and service to society, Gurudev said, "Keep doing what you are doing now. What better gift could Swami Vivekananda's mother have given the world?" What comforting and inspiring words for women!

Pūjya Gurudev conducted *Gītā* jñāna-yajñas tirelessly. My uncle once attended a *Gītā* jñāna-yajña by Gurudev in Bengaluru. One of his friends asked, "What is the use of giving lectures on the *Gītā*? How is it helpful to people?" My uncle replied, "By teaching the *Gītā*, Swamiji is taking us closer to eternal happiness. By following His teachings, we can get over our miseries in life." This was the impact of Gurudev's teachings on His audience. Gurudev just did not preach the *Bhagavad-gītā* but lived the *Gītā* every moment as 'suhṛdaṁ sarvabhūtānām' (a well-wisher of all).

The Chinmaya Mission Pledge, written by Gurudev, reflects the universal vision of oneness. We all need a well-wisher in life. If we follow Pūjya Gurudev's advice, we do not need another well-wisher in our lives. As a well-wisher of all, He advised, "Do just as Mother Ganga does every time she comes down from the white peaks of the Himalayas to serve the whole of mankind." As we chant the Chinmaya Mission Pledge, "May thy grace and blessings flow through us to the world around us," let us pray that we become inspired to become well-wishers of society just like our Pūjya Gurudev.

eṣa sarveśvaraḥ eṣa sarvajñaḥ eṣo'ntaryāmyeṣaḥ,
yoniḥ sarvasya prabhavāpyayau hi bhūtānām.

This is the Lord of all, this is the knower of all, this is the inner controller, this is the source of all. And this is that from which all things originate and in which they finally dissolve themselves.

~ *Mandukyopanishad* 6

97

Om Satyasaṅkalpāya Namaḥ

Salutations to the one who is of true resolve.

Suresh Ramakrishnan

Satya saṅkalpa, as described, directly translates to 'true resolve'. In the context of Pūjya Gurudev Swami Chinmayananda, for any resolution taken, everything will be done to ensure it is fulfilled. Throughout Gurudev's lifetime, He managed to take on a plethora of tasks initially deemed either futile or unattainable. Despite this, if it was His wish, it inevitably came true.

While studying Vedānta under Swami Tapovan Maharaj in the Himalayas, Gurudev decided He wanted to share His newfound knowledge with the world and, through time and dedication, was able to swiftly gain a large following, leading to what we know today as our beloved Chinmaya Mission. He also established the Sandeepany Sadhanalaya, which is unique to the Chinmaya Mission through which His saṅkalpa has continued and will continue for generations through our swāmins, brahmacārins, and each one of us.

Another saṅkalpa of Gurudev was that of the famed statue of Hanumānji and a temple of Śrī Rāma at His āśram in Sidhbari. The story goes as follows: While attempting to build an āśram in Sidhbari, the scaffolding often fell due to the high winds in this area of Himachal Pradesh. Many told Gurudev that building any structure there would be impossible. His response? "Build a thirty-foot Hanumānji statue; do not worry, all will be okay." To the surprise of all those present, following the installation of the Hanumanji statue, the āśram and Śrī Rāma temple were built swiftly without any further problems. The task was completed simply by His conviction, His saṅkalpa.

This saṅkalpa of His can be found in recent history with the establishment of Chinmaya Vishwa Vidyapeeth! Gurudev once proclaimed, prior to His earthly departure, His intent to establish a university within India that merges conventional and Indian knowledge systems. Though it has taken some time, His saṅkalpa has manifested in our University, which will continue to grow!

This almighty name reflects the ideation that every thought Gurudev entertained manifested as a saṅkalpa, and therefore, to document all examples of His 'satya saṅkalpa' nature would be impossible. Every devotee who has been associated with Gurudev can share their personal experience to reaffirm this truth.

Finally, Gurudev has taken the saṅkalpa that He is waiting for each one of us to join Him, and together, we will all cross over to the other shore. Gurudev's presence is still very much with us, so let's put our best efforts into joining Him as quickly as possible.

"If a seeker is steady in his sādhana and can still maintain his divine urge to know and to become, if he is passionate enough to reject and renounce even the powers and joys of Godhood, he during the highest flights of his deepest meditation, wafts even beyond the yonder summits of sattva, and becomes sattvātīta, or one who has transcended even the gods. He experiences in himself the supreme Truth and becomes That. Having reached Om and merging in Om, he becomes Om."

~ Swami Chinmayananda

98

Om Santuṣṭāya Namaḥ

Salutations to the content one.

Sushma Siva

Every one of us is trying to find happiness through impermanent things. We are helplessly caught in the fast race of life in the consumption-based world. Our neighborhoods often see delivery trucks full of merchandise dropping off 'impermanent happiness'! Amusingly enough, the trucks have a sign, "Warning: contents may cause happiness." To add to this comedy, these trucks are loaded in places called fulfillment centers! But what can provide lasting fulfillment is rarely understood. This is where Pūjya Gurudev's works come to guide the seekers of Truth.

We are all very fortunate to have Gurudev show us the path to true permanent happiness, which is both sustainable and rewarding. Gurudev gifted us with the Body-Mind-Intellect (BMI) chart by translating what the ṛṣis of yore saw through their subtle vision. This simple yet comprehensive tool is a brilliant model that helps us discriminate the subjective Real and Blissful aspects from the objective, turbulent worldly experiences. He taught us that instead of depending on the constantly changing external world, the source of true and permanent happiness can be found by fine-tuning the instrument we already have.

Gurudev showed us that true fulfillment does not lead to inaction but is a product of higher standards and ideals. From the foothills of the Himalayas, just like Mother Ganga enthusiastically rushes down to serve all lives in her way, Swamiji came down to the valleys to share the divine secret with the masses. Every moment with Him was jubilant, enthusiastic, dynamic, peaceful, and inspiring. Irrespective of the conditions, He would find a way to reach maximum efficiency, whether in a chilled, air-conditioned room or outside in the dusty, sweltering heat. By temperament, a karma yogī, He was 'ātmanyevātmanā tuṣṭaḥ', reveling in His true Self. He is the lighthouse to millions of seekers.

Transcending existing boundaries of social structure and biases, He introduced nontraditional ways of teaching and spreading the scriptures. Many are now taken for granted but were revolutionary and controversial when Gurudev first introduced them. Endowed with courage and conviction, He would attract and transform even the most disinterested with His infectious warmth, ready wit, and dynamism. This is the power of working out of fulfillment. This can happen only with a Mahātmā out of fullness of heart and wisdom.

Having disentangled all the knots of the heart, namely, ignorance, desire, and desire-driven actions, shattered all doubts into smithereens, and all karmas burnt asunder, He apprehended the Reality of Infinitude. Above all, having transcended His BMI and ego identifications, He tirelessly worked for more than four decades, giving maximum happiness to the maximum number of people.

99

Om Sādhave Namaḥ

Salutations to the pious one.

Swapna Nayar

In the *Bhagavad-gītā*, Śrī Ādi Śankarācārya describes 'sādhu' as a good and pious person who follows the scriptures and lives a virtuous life. We find these qualities in Pūjya Gurudev. Ever since He got the 'Knowledge of the Self' in the Himalayas, His life was transformed. He felt that this precious knowledge should be spread all over the world so that people can benefit. He taught the *Bhagavad-gītā* to millions throughout His life and showed us how to live in this world. He followed the teachings of our scriptures, led a virtuous life, and demonstrated this to others.

Gosvāmī Tulasīdāsa describes the character of a sādhu in *Rāmacaritamānasa*:

sādhu carit subh carit kapāsu,
niras bisad guṇamay phal jāsu.

"The story of sādhus is like that of cotton – pure and full of good qualities and detached."

Cotton is white, pure, and has many threads. Similarly, a sādhu is sāttvik and has many qualities. Cotton undergoes a lot of pain till it is converted into cloth. After that, it is cut by scissors and again sewn by needle to make clothing to cover our body. Pūjya Gurudev patiently listened to the sorrows and sufferings of devotees, consoled them, gave them advice, and instructed them to follow sādhana as per scriptures. He sometimes took their pain as well. He underwent a lot of hardship to gain the knowledge of the Self and then spent His entire life blessing the world. He removed the negativities of many and instilled positive values. His teachings covered all, from the womb to the tomb.

In *Śrīmad Bhāgavatam*, Kapila Muni describes to His mother, Devahūtī, the qualities of a sādhu and the glory of 'sādhu saṅga' (company of sādhu), which can liberate a person. Kapila Muni says, "The characteristics of a sādhu are that he is tolerant, merciful, and friendly to all living entities. He has no enemies, he is peaceful, and he abides by the scriptures. These are sādhu's ornaments" (canto 3.25.21). "Such a sādhu engages in firm devotional services to the Lord without deviation. For the sake of the Lord, he renounces all other connections, such as family relationships and friendly acquaintances" (canto 3.25.22). "Engaging constantly in chanting and hearing about Me, the Supreme, the sādhus do not suffer from material miseries because they are filled with thoughts of my stories." (canto 3.25.23). Bhagavān Kapila advises His mother, Devahūtī, to be in the company of such a holy person.

We find all these qualities in our Pūjya Gurudev. We have experienced many instances of His patience, mercy, grace, and care for all living entities. His bhakti towards Jagadīśvara was evident in every action. Throughout His life, He sang the divine teachings of Lord Kṛṣṇa and spread the knowledge of Advaita Vedānta. The more we listen to His discourses on the *Bhagavad-gītā*, Upaniṣad, and other texts, and stories from the fortunate devotees who came into His contact, we find these qualities in full measure in Pūjya Gurudev.

100

Om Sumanase Namaḥ

Salutations to the one who has a good mind.

Brahmacharini Vaani I. Ramkhalawan

'Su-manas' can simply be translated as 'good mind'. Pūjya Gurudev's ceaseless and unwavering love for mankind was a luminous reflection of that which was within Him – a magnanimous heart, a beautiful mind.

Goodness is naturally inherent, in varying degrees, in all living beings. It is that which brings beauty to intentions, thoughts, and actions. The enlightened Master, Pūjya Gurudev Swami Chinmayananda, stood above all because of His pure mind and kind-hearted spirit. This was evident in His every living breath, and the effects are still felt years after His mahāsamādhi.

This world was His altar onto which He offered flowers in the form of auspicious thoughts. A renowned authority on Upaniṣads and *Bhagavad-gītā*, this great ṛṣi, who was referred to as the Swami Vivekananda of the twentieth century, brought an awakening! His adaptability to being relevant inspired many towards self-transformation. Pūjya Gurudev lived a life in full awareness of all. Undaunted by the adversities of life, He was ever cheerful! His benevolence was limitless, and His actions were channeled through His vision of maximum benefit for all.

Pūjya Guruji, Swami Tejomayananda, spoke of His master's kindness, "Gurudev's greatness went beyond His presence, which He showed in every little thing. In big things, everybody shows off. But Gurudev showed it even in small things."

Many of us have not met Pūjya Gurudev in this physical realm, yet this Mahātmā continues to touch lives! Those who have been touched by His grace experience the effects!

To bear witness to the endearing and unending energy of my Guru, Swami Prakashananda, in adoration and fulfillment of the grand vision of His master at our center in Trinidad and Tobago, provided the impetus for many of us to serve. Here at our Sandeepany Sadhanalaya āśram in Mumbai, I witnessed the most incredible gift He gave to mankind – empowerment and transformation through the wisdom of Vedānta. His noble intentions were recorded clearly in the minutes of meetings with the Board of Trustees – Knowledge for all. He may not have seen all come to fruition. Still, His thoughts, in the form of saṅkalpas, bore fruit through the untiring efforts and inexhaustible love of our Pūjya Guruji Swami Tejomayananda, Pūjya Swami Swaroopananda, and the innumerable sevaks.

From Shishu Vihar to Bala Vihar, to Chinmaya Yuva Kendra (CHYK), from the Chinmaya Vidyalayas in and out of Bhārat, to an International Residential School, to an International Research Foundation, to the Sandeepany Sadhanalayas – there was no exception to any age group. We are now seeing the blossoming of Chinmaya Vishwa Vidyapeeth, the only de-novo university – with a unique approach incorporating Indian knowledge systems in academia. Our salutations to this great saint, whose thoughts pervade the dust of Bhārat and the world at large and will continue for many generations.

101

Om Suhṛde Namaḥ

Salutations to the one who has a good heart.

Swami Deveshananda

Pūjya Gurudev Swami Sri Chinmayananda was a true friend and well-wisher of all beings. Just like Śrī Kṛṣṇa protected Arjuna and the cowherd boys, Gurudev loves and blesses His devotees, protects them, gives them joy, and liberates them. Pūjya Gurudev is also our true friend (suhṛd), a benevolent well-wisher who always guides us.

Whenever we faced challenges in life, Pūjya Gurudev helped us through His teachings. He encouraged and appreciated everyone. He was selfless and dispassionate. He forgave easily and was always kind to all. He was impartial and ignored our imperfections. Hence, He was a suhṛd of all.

Gurudev was always there to take care of whoever surrendered totally to Him. I have experienced this several times. Whenever we undertook big projects and fell short of volunteers, Gurudev's grace brought those extra pairs of hands needed to make the project successful! In 1993, Pūjya Gurudev did a jñāna-yajña on chapter six of the *Bhagavad-gītā* in Vadodara. After the yajña, He met with the youth group. He said to them, "Whenever you face challenges in life, close your eyes, see Lord Nārāyaṇa within your heart, and seek His guidance. But always remember that you are only an instrument in His hand."

Pūjya Gurudev was immaculate and pure. He was a great Master, Guru, well-wisher, visionary, and a true friend. He was a living embodiment of the Vedik wisdom and dedicated His life to spreading the message of the scriptures. He realized His true calling was serving humanity as a spiritual teacher. He traveled around the world, gave discourses, and taught the *Bhagavad-gītā*, the Upaniṣads, and other sacred texts. He also authored several books on a variety of spiritual topics. He founded several educational institutions, including the Chinmaya Vidyalayas, and Chinmaya Vishwa Vidyapeeth, a university in India that merges conventional and Indian knowledge systems. He also established the Chinmaya Mission Hospitals, which provide free medical care to the poor.

Gurudev was a source of strength and inspiration. He always encouraged His devotees to live a life of love, peace, purpose, and harmony.

Gurudev will be remembered for His wisdom, wit, humor, compassion, and dedication. He was a living example of how to live a life of love and compassion, and He will continue to inspire people for generations to come.

One of Gurudev's most famous sayings was, "Strive, strive, and strive till you win. Never look back and go ahead." This saying is a reminder that we should never give up on our dreams, no matter how difficult they may seem. We should always keep moving forward and never give up on our goals.

Gurudev has also taught us the importance of sādhana (spiritual practice). He said that sādhana is the key to realizing our true Self. Gurudev's words of wisdom are a valuable gift to the world. We should all strive to follow His example and live our lives to the fullest. Pūjya Gurudev has always guided, blessed, and encouraged us in many ways. We prostrate at the feet of such a great Guru!

102

Om Svayaṁ-jyotiṣe Namaḥ

Salutations to the Self-effulgent one.

Veena Venkatesh

This nāmāvali of Pūjya Gurudev indicates His Divine nature. Jyoti means light, and svayaṁ jyoti means Self-illuminating, also called svayaṁ prakāśa, which stands for that ever-shining Consciousness principle.

In every Hindu household, we start our daily worship with the lighting of a lamp before the deity in the prayer room. All auspicious functions, religious as well as social, commence with the lighting of the lamp. As we all know, the Chinmaya Mission logo is a lamp that symbolizes knowledge. The oil lamp in the logo represents the ethical life needed to light the flame of knowledge within.

It is important to know that a single lamp can light hundreds of others, just as a single Realized Master like our Pūjya Gurudev has enlightened millions! Despite sharing its light with other lamps, the original lamp does not lose its brilliance. In the same way, sharing knowledge with others will not diminish our jñāna; instead, it enhances our clarity. While performing ārati, we chant a śloka that describes the light of all lights – "There the sun does not shine, nor does the moon nor the stars. There this lightning does not shine, what to talk of this fire? That alone is (ever) shining. All shine after Him who shines. By the light of That alone, all this is illuminated."

Śrī Ādi Śankarācārya encapsulates the philosophy of

Vedānta in a single śloka called ekaśloki, which is written as a dialogue between a teacher and his student. The meaning of the śloka goes like this:

"Is it your light that shines in the day as the sun and as the bright lamp in the night? What is the light that shines when I close my eyes? What is that light that illumines my intellectual perception? You are that supreme light that illumines the awareness of 'ahaṃ', and I am that light. In short, 'that thou art' or 'ahaṃ brahmāsmi'. I am that by the light of which the world is illumined in the day and the night because Brahman is the source of all light, Agni or Sūrya. He is the light through which the indriyas function. When the eyes are closed and there is no perception, then the mind functions with the help of the intellect, which in turn functions by the light of the Ātman, which is beyond body, mind, and intellect, and that am I, the supreme Reality, Brahman. In this light of knowledge and wisdom, a spiritual seeker is able to discern truth from falsehood, good from bad, and permanent reality from the impermanent world."

Pūjya Gurudev is that light of Consciousness in our world who is illuminating all our experiences. That Chinmaya Jyoti guides us in our spiritual journey. To rediscover that Divinity within us, a mature sādhaka would say, tamaso mā jyotir gamaya (Lead me from darkness to light. Lead me from ignorance to knowledge). Ignorance, like darkness, obscures our true understanding. Just like the only remedy for darkness is light, the only remedy for ignorance is the knowledge of the Self, ātma-jñāna. Let that Chinmaya Jyoti help guide us and keep glowing within us.

103

Om Sthitaprajñāya Namaḥ

Salutations to the one who is established in the highest wisdom.

Venkatesh Hollabbi

When you chant this name of Pūjya Gurudev, a question arises in the mind of the sādhaka (seeker). What is the destination on the spiritual highway? Who has reached that destination? How does he behave? How does he act? The same questions were asked by Arjuna in *Śrīmad Bhagavad-gītā* (2.54).

Sthitaprajña: 'sthita' means to be firmly established or rooted in; 'prajñā' generally means intellect, however, in the current context it means 'consciousness'. In simple words, prajñā is jñāna (knowledge/wisdom), which is Consciousness. In short, sthitaprajña refers to a man of steady wisdom and equipoise, rooted in the knowledge of the Self (ātma-jñāna) or merged with that Supreme Brahman. Bhagavān Śrī Kṛṣṇa gives further answers in ślokas 2.55-2.72 of *the Bhagavad-gītā.* These indicators of one who knows the supreme Self (ātma-jñāni lakṣaṇas) serve as the benchmark for the seekers.

In verse 2.55, Bhagavān Kṛṣṇa says that the one who has reached that stage of desirelessness is ever reveling and content in his true Self. He is equipoised and maintains equanimity. He does not hanker after pleasures, has rejected both bāhya viṣaya (external pursuits) and bhoga viṣaya (objects of pleasure) and is free from attachment, fear, and anger. Such a sage is known as sthitaprajña, the man absorbed constantly in Brahman.

An often-quoted verse from *Bhaja Govindam* (20) to describe this jīvanmukta lakṣaṇa or the indicators of one who knows the Supreme Self reinforces this idea:

Yoga rato vā – he is reveling in yoga (union with Lord); bhoga rato vā – he revels in enjoyment if it comes to him; sanga rato vā – takes delight in company; sanga vihīnaḥ – bereft of company or in solitude; yasya – for whom; cittam – the mind; ramatē brahmaṇi – is reveling in Brahman; nandati nandati nandatyēva – he delights and enjoys. He is reveling in that absolute state of fulfillment.

The *Bhagavad-gītā* calls such a person sthitaprajña, a man of realization, jīvanmukta puruṣaḥ. Jīvanmukta literally means liberated while living. He is enjoying the brāhmisthiti – that Absolute peace! This is ātma-jñāna phalam, the prayojana, the result of Self-knowledge. The sādhaka has reached his destination! Bandha has become the Buddha, and mānava has become the Mādhava. This is the journey of the sādhaka from a life of mamatā (egocentric) to samatā (Godcentric) to pūrnatā (a life of fulfillment).

Having known this highest Knowledge, there is nothing more to know. Jīvanmukta is one who has a firm conviction that I am Existence-Consciousness-Bliss. This is effortless awareness for Him. This firm conviction comes due to the strength of His knowledge. This awareness for an ātma-jñāni is unbroken, spontaneous, and natural. He lives only for the general welfare of others.

We owe a debt of gratitude to our Pūjya Gurudev, who had a transformational effect on our lives with His teachings. He tirelessly worked to benefit the entire humanity with this ancient wisdom and simplifying the treasures of Vedānta.

104

Om Kṣamāśīlāya Namaḥ

Salutations to the forgiving one.

Vijay Gupta

To err is human, and forgiveness is Divine. Pūjya Gurudev was so large-hearted that He didn't even take offense in the first place. His way of expressing kṣamā (forgiveness) was unique. It was a lesson, a reward, and a memory to be cherished forever. May we see the oneness in all and be naturally forgiving like Gurudev.

Once, at the end of a jñāna-yajña of Pūjya Gurudev, a devotee stole all the Guru-dakṣiṇa. Everybody criticized this person. The devotee later realized his wrongdoing, returned the Guru-dakṣiṇa, and apologized to Gurudev. Pūjya Gurudev smiled and unconditionally accepted his apology as though nothing happened. Pūjya Gurudev, being perfect, would know what to tell each disciple to make them perfect. He endured all mistakes compassionately. He covered the disciples' defects without highlighting them. Pūjya Gurudev explained that misunderstanding is easy, but understanding is difficult and needs maturity. He further explained that if someone has done something wrong, put yourself in that person's shoes to clearly understand his situation. That helps us to forgive through reasoning.

When Pūjya Gurudev started giving discourses in English, many paṇḍits criticized and cursed in various ways. They complained to Shri Shankaracharya that this svāmī is an unreligious person and should not be allowed to give discourses. Shri Shankaracharya pacified them by saying that Gurudev's teachings are pure and correct. Pūjya Gurudev did not take offense and did not alienate them, and many of the paṇḍits who criticized became His disciples.

Pūjya Gurudev explained that kṣamā is one of the greatest qualities one can possess. He explained forgiveness as a voluntary act of letting go of the hurt, anger, and negative feelings towards another who has offended oneself. Forgiveness is like the fragrance that is left behind by crushed leaves of the Tulasī plant on the fingers that destroyed them in a thoughtless act. He further said, sandalwood perfumes, even the axe that hurls it down! The more we rub sandalwood against a stone, the more its fragrance spreads. Burn it, and it wafts its glory through the entire neighborhood – such is the enchanting beauty of forgiveness in life.

Pūjya Gurudev explains that forgiveness is important because when we forgive, there is immediate peace. Otherwise, we burn in the fire of revenge, anger, and hatred night and day. "God gives and forgives. Man gets and forgets." The person might have hurt you once. For life, you constantly hurt yourself by remembering it repeatedly. Seek forgiveness from the Lord for all the conscious and unconscious errors that you may have made, and forgive everyone every night before you sleep.

To forgive others' imperfections unconditionally is a rare quality. Our Pūjya Gurudev, who was perfect and established in the highest wisdom, was a kṣamāśīla!

105

Om Jñānamūrtaye Namaḥ

Salutations to the embodiment of Knowledge.

Vijay Kumar

This mantra is often used to express devotion, reverence, and respect for the divine source of knowledge and wisdom. The term jñāna-mūrti refers to the one who embodies knowledge and enlightenment. Pūjya Gurudev was rooted in knowledge. He focused His teachings mainly on the *Bhagavad-gītā* and Upaniṣads. He established simple methods of teaching the highest Knowledge and continuously encouraged people to walk the path of knowledge. "Live Vedānta, and thus let us reach 'That' destination where having met, we shall never part. Meet me there. Reach there through love, service, and purity." This was His teaching.

Why were Gurudev's talks called jñāna-yajña? Traditionally, yajña is a joint sacrificial endeavor for the society's welfare, as explained in the *Bhagavad-gītā*. Gurudev took the concept of jñāna-yajña to a higher level, where people contributed in terms of time, effort, and money to organize yajñas, and He offered knowledge. His talks kindled and set ablaze the fire of knowledge. Thus, the supreme Knowledge was made freely available.

He conducted more than 500 jñāna-yajñas in India and abroad. He could explain the most profound truth even to a child. He was established in the Knowledge of the Self. In the *Gītā*, Śrī Kṛṣṇa says that out of all the yajñas, jñāna-yajña is the highest. Gurudev's strength was knowledge, and He operated in the world from that standpoint. He said, "For the first time, I tasted bliss in meditation, which I know is an iota of what one can have from deep, long, steady, and powerful meditation. My only prayer to my Guru and to the Lord is that, by their grace, may I never fall and may I drink deeper at the fountain of eternal Divine nectar!"

Jñāna-yajña is a word coined by Śrī Vedavyāsa that means 'sacrifice in knowledge'. As a result of the study of scriptures, some fresh ideas and healthy values rise in us. Into that fire of knowledge, all old false ideas are burned down. Gurudev says that we who have not burnt our old false ideas don't see things as they are. We see things as we are – colored by our views and opinions based on our mind and intellect. Then, we make decisions and judgments, and we classify, categorize, compare, and analyze with our knowledge about the world. We then say we are 'right', which is a contradiction! Only a jñāni sees the world as it is.

Why is so much importance given to knowledge? Bhagavān says, "Certainly there is no purifier in this world, like Knowledge. He who is himself perfected in yoga finds it in the Self, in time." (*Bhagavad-gītā* 4.38) Knowledge is not merely acquiring more information. The information gathered must be put to practical use. Giving up old methods of living and taking up new creative ways of living is jñāna-yajña.

His teachings made it clear that knowledge is superior to experience. For example, we experience sunrises and sunsets, which are very beautiful. But in reality, the earth rotates; the sun neither rises nor sets. Similarly, this changing world, though appears real, is illusory. But we are not ready to accept it. Let us all live without compromises, discard old habits and be firm in the path shown by our beloved Gurudev, Swami Chinmayananda!

106

Om Jñānayōgine Namaḥ

Salutations to the one who attained the goal (Reality) through the path of Knowledge.

Swami Nirbhayananda

Humor and stories are the most fascinating things that hold a child's attention. My fond memories of Pūjya Gurudev start with a humorous joke I heard from him at the age of six, sitting with my father in Pūjya Gurudev's yajñaśālā.

The story was of a small boy who used to break toys the very next day after his father brought them home. One day, the boy's father brought an unbreakable toy for his son. The next day, as his father returned, he was happy to see that his son was still playing with the toy. But to his utter dismay, as he walked into his home, he noticed that the little boy had broken the beautiful clay items in the showcase.

Everyone laughed at this joke as they all could relate to such incidents in their homes. Gurudev paused and roared, "The little boy was inquisitive; with his little knowledge, he performed his experiments. Knowledge is the source of all expressions and all action." Years later, my father told me, "See how, with a simple example, He explained the need for the right knowledge."

Pūjya Gurudev was a jñāna yogī, a living embodiment of Absolute Knowledge. He was never working for Himself or to project His ideas. He used to say, "I am just opening the works of Bhagavān Ādi Śankara."

Gurudev's mind was always absorbed in the knowledge

absolute. He had no attachment to the world, but at the same time, His care for Īśvara's creation was seen as the best. This could, for example, be seen in the simple acts of everyday life, such as opening an envelope and still allowing the beauty of the envelope to remain intact.

One day, during a satsaṅg, Gurudev was asked about the audience of His yajña. His reply was, "Narāyaṇa is speaking to Narāyaṇa alone." Gurudev was a Mahātmā because He experienced the whole world as Narāyaṇa, the Truth, which is Existence-Consciousness-Bliss.

It is difficult to find people who are large-hearted, but rarer still is to find those who can accommodate everyone, and it is very rare indeed to find one who realizes the Truth that pervades the universe and thus becomes the All-Pervading Truth.

There is a famous story that represents the Truth. A man in a group of ten people was searching for the last tenth man when a wise man walked in, showing him to be the tenth man. The man had forgotten to count himself! Gurudev was like that wise man who showed us our true Self through absolute Knowledge.

Gurudev taught us, "We are the Infinite Truth" (tattvamasi). Until and unless the knowledge thought "I am the Infinite Truth" (akhaṇḍākāra vṛtti) takes place in the mind of the disciple, he is not liberated.

107

Om Jñānatṛptāya Namaḥ

Salutations to the one who is content in the Knowledge of the Self.

Swami Sarvagananda

Pūjya Gurudev's name itself denotes that He is full of knowledge. Cinmayaḥ is Cit+mayaḥ, which is the same as jñāna mayaḥ.

As stated in *Muṇḍaka-upaniṣad*, there are two kinds of knowledge to acquire: parā and aparā – the higher and the lower. The higher knowledge, parā vidyā, leads to immortality or goes beyond the word meaning in languages, popularly known as Sat-Cit-Ānanda.

In *Pañcadaśī*, tṛpti dīpa prakaraṇa, Śrī Vidyāraṇya Swāmi explains what tṛpti (contentment) is. Verse 7.32 of this text says that having been taught by a Sadguru and analyzing on his own, all sorrows experienced as a result of thinking that 'I am the doer, I am the enjoyer' left him. He feels that he has done whatever has to be done and attained whatever has to be attained, and he rejoices in joyful jñāna, which is called tṛpti – obtained on getting established in brahma jñāna. Verse 7.47 says that after the elimination of all saṃsāra by the experience of the Truth, which is ever-free, unrestricted contentment arises. This is called 'niratiśaya ānandarūpa tṛpti'; in other words, it is the only state where there is only complete contentment – tṛpti. And Pūjya Gurudev was fully content with Brahmavidyā or Self Knowledge.

Observing Gurudev's works, we see the confluence of

four mighty masters in Him – Bhagavān Śrī Vedavyāsa, Śrī Ādi Śankarācārya, Śrī Vidyāraṇya Swāmi, and Pūjya Swami Tapovan Maharaj.

Gurudev was a powerful orator, the author of the world-acclaimed commentary on the *Bhagavad-gītā*, and a super administrator. He was the creative mind behind beautiful temples and āśrams – Sandeepany Sadhanalaya in Mumbai, Vana Sitarama Temple, Veera Hanuman at Chinmaya Tapovan āśram in Sidhbari, Tapovan Kuti in Uttarkashi, and Spatikalinga temple at Tamaraipakkam in Chennai to name a few. Further, Gurudev inspired the construction of several Chinmaya Vidyalayas and Chinmaya Mission centers across the globe, the Chinmaya Organisation for Rural Development, a nurses training program in Sidhbari, and a Chinmaya Mission Hospital in Bengaluru. He also started the Sandeepany Sadhanalaya, Vedānta Seminary in English in Mumbai, now conducted in Hindi in Sidhbari and other regional languages in different states. His vision is continuing to manifest as Chinmaya International Residential School and Chinmaya Vishwa Vidyapeeth.

When a sādhaka comes into contact with Gurudev, the mumukṣutvam dormant within is kindled and made to dominate that personality.

I came into contact with Him in 1978-79, during one of His yajñas in Coimbatore. His discourses were transformative for His listeners. All endeavors aim at changing and reviving the cultural fabric of the country. There is no end to His glories. Without any expectations in return, He shared His immense Bliss that eternally flowed from within Him. Salutations to this Great Mahātmā!

108

Om Nitya-Śuddha-Buddha -Mukta Svarūpāya Namaḥ

Salutations to the one who is the nature of the eternal, pure, and liberated.

Vivek Gupta

Many years ago, a publisher asked me to describe Pūjya Gurudev, Swami Chinmayananda in one word, and the word that came to me was – wizard.

Think about what kinds of associations the single word wizard evokes – majestic and charismatic, powerful and peaceful, magical and mystical. I still think of Gurudev as a wizard, though years later, I feel He is exponentially more of a – savior.

Think about what kinds of associations the single word savior evokes – the one, the only one, who can save in a fundamental way. Gurudev is accurately praised as nitya-śuddha-buddha-mukta svarūpa – shared simply, one who has transcended smallness (vāsanā nāśa). You can only share what you have. If I have food, I can share food. If I have time, I can share time. If I have vāsanās, I tend to spread vāsanās. Gurudev did not have vāsanās, and so was the only one who could share how to be free (mukta) without vāsanās.

I often ask students – What is the greatest gift you can give your parents? Most, introspectively say, time. Few rightly share – not having them worry about me. Giving this greatest gift is only possible if the child does not have worries.

In this reflection, try to feel the gift that Gurudev has offered to us. Through the example of His life and the eloquence of His teachings, we know how to be free of SADness (stress-anxiety-dejection) – a gift to ourselves, a gift to our parents, a gift to all generations. Only a savior can manifest such a gift.

Om nitya-śuddha-buddha-mukta svarūpāya namaḥ: Gurudev is a savior:

- at a causal level, He is reducing humanity's smallness
- at a subtle level, He is reducing humanity's SADness
- at a gross level, He is giving himself to humanity through Chinmaya Mission.

As a Śiṣya (disciple) of the thirteenth Vedanta Course at Sandeepany Sadhanalaya from September 2005 – September 2007, with Guruji, Swami Tejomayananda as the Ācārya, I have viscerally felt Him reach into my heart and chip away at what I am not – smallness, SAD-ness, and so on. This experience is most painful and relieving (mukta).

I bow my head to the feet of Gurudev and Guruji for saving me, for making me.

"He was – He is – He will be, forever harnessing our minds, guiding our intellects, softening our hearts and serving through our hands, our beloved Gurudev, unfailingly treasured in the deepest recesses of our Beings as Pure Love!"
~ Source: Chinmaya Ashtottara Namavali, Chinmaya YouTube Channel

THE mananam SERIES

(Mananam – Sanskrit for 'Reflection upon the Truth')

Prior publications listed in sequence (most recent listed first)

Reincarnation: The Karmic Cycle
Heal-Thy Self: A Holistic Approach to Health and Well-being
Youth: Keeping the Balance (Revised Edition)
Vignettes of Resilience: Hindu Spiritual Care for Healing from Loss
Values in the Workplace (Revised Edition)
Egocentric to Ecocentric: From Conflict to Coexistence
The Sages Speak About Immortality (Revised Edition)
Am I That I Am?: Exploring Identity Crisis
Tuning to God
Many Problems: ONE Solution
Exceeding Excellence
Beyond Change
Getting Out of the Box: Living a Whole Life
Keeping the Rhythm: Role of Self-Effort in Destiny
Prayer
Divine Purpose
Truth
Life is a Gift: Living is an Art
Guru: The Guiding Light
Values in the Work Place
Living in the Present
Compassion
Fear: Face It
Education: Toward Inner Transformation
The Science of Sciences
Youth: Keeping the Balance
In the Company of Sages

THE **mananam** SERIES

The list of prior publications contd...

Peace in a Restless World
Mananam: Reflection Upon the Truth
Devotion
Emotions
Service: An Act of Worship
Vision of the Bhagavad Gita
The Journey Called Life
The Light of Wisdom
Reincarnation: The Karmic Cycle
Maya: The Divine Power
Embracing Love
At Home in the Universe
Beyond Ego
Happiness Through Integration
Living in Simplicity
Timeless Values
The Path of Love
Mind: Our Greatest Gift
The Sages Speak About Immortality
The Sages Speak About Life & Death
Divine Songs: The Gitas of India
Religion and Spirituality
Time and Beyond
About Sadhana
Divine Grace
Spirituality in Family Life
The Divine Mother
Beyond Stress
The Power of Faith
Joy: Our True Nature
Contemplation in a World of Action
Love and Forgiveness
Saints and Mystics
Om: The Symbol of Truth
The Illusory Ego
The Source of Inspiration
The Essential Teacher
The Razor's Edge
Harmony and Beauty
The Question of Freedom
The Pursuit of Happiness
On the Path
Beyond Sorrow
Self-Discovery
The Mystery of Creation
Vedanta in Action
Solitude

Transliteration and Pronunciation Guide

In the book, Devanāgarī characters are transliterated according to the scheme adopted by the International Congress of Orientalists at Athens in 1912. In it, one fixed pronunciation value is given to each letter; f, q, w, x, and z are not called to use. An audio recording of this guide is available at www.chinmayamission.com/scriptures.php. According to this scheme:

	sounds like		*sounds like*
´	a silent 'a'	l	l in *l*ove
a	o in s*o*n	ḷ	**
ā	a in f*a*ther	m	m in *m*ind
ai	i in del*i*ght	ṁ	m in *im*provise
au	o in n*o*w	n	n in *n*ose
b	b in *b*oil	ṅ	an in *an*kle*
bh	bh in a*bh*or	ṇ	n in *un*der*
c	ch in *ch*uckle	ñ	ny in ba*ny*an
ch	ch in it*ch**	o	o in c*o*re
d	th in *th*is	p	p in *p*en
ḍ	d in *d*og	ph	ph in *ph*antom*
dh	dh in Gan*dh*i	r	r in *r*ight
ḍh	dh in a*dh*esive	ṛ	rh in r*hy*thm*
e	a in ev*a*de	ṝ	**
g	g in *g*ate	s	in *s*imple
gh	gh in *gh*ost	ṣ	in *s*ugar
h	h in *h*appy	ś	sh in *sh*ut
ḥ	**	t	t in *t*abla
i	i in d*i*fferent	ṭ	t in *t*ank
ī	ee in f*ee*t	th	th in *th*umb
j	j in *j*ust	ṭh	**
jh	jh in *Jh*ansi	tr	th in *th*ree*
jñ	gn in *gn*osis	u	u in f*u*ll
k	c in *c*alm	ū	oo in b*oo*t
kh	kh in *kh*an	v	v in *v*ery
kṣ	tio in ac*tio*n	y	y in *y*es

* These letters do not have an exact English equivalent. An approximation is given here.

** These sounds cannot be approximated in English words.

About Mananam

The Sanskrit word mananam means "reflection." The Mananam Series of books is dedicated to promoting the ageless wisdom of Vedānta, with an emphasis on the unity of all religions. Spiritual teachers from different traditions give us fresh, insightful answers to age-old questions so that we may apply them in practical ways to the dilemmas we all face in life. Mananam is published twice yearly by Chinmaya Mission West, which was founded by Swami Chinmayananda in 1975.

Swami Chinmayananda pursued the spiritual path in the Himalayas under the guidance of Swami Sivananda and Swami Tapovan. He is credited with the awakening of India and the rest of the world to the ageless wisdom of Vedānta. He taught the logic of spirituality and emphasized that selfless work, study, and meditation are the cornerstones of spiritual practice. His legacy remains in the form of books, audio and video recordings, schools, social service projects, and Vedānta teachers, who now serve their local communities all around the world.

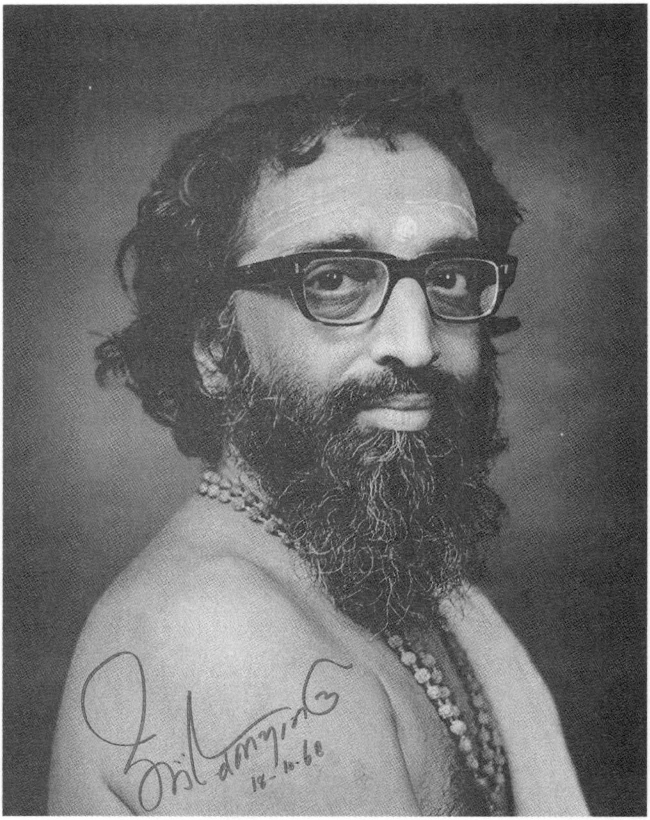
18-10-68